JUDSON PRESS
PUBLISHERS SINCE 1824

Church Programs & Celebrations for All Generations

Rachel Gilmore

JUDSON PRESS
PUBLISHERS SINCE 1824
VALLEY FORGE, PA

Church Programs and Celebrations for All Generations
© 2010 by Judson Press, Valley Forge, PA 19482-0851

Interior design by Beth Oberholtzer.
Cover design by The Signal Hill Company, LLC.

Library of Congress Cataloging-in-Publication Data
Gilmore, Rachel.
    Church programs & celebrations for all generations / Rachel Gilmore.
      p. cm.
    ISBN 978-0-8170-1642-5 (pbk. : alk. paper) 1. Worship programs. I. Title.
II. Title: Church programs and celebrations for all generations.

BV198.G55   2010
264—dc22

                              2010015260

Printed in the U.S.A.
First Edition, 2010.

To my mom, Karen Maurer, who taught me firsthand about experiential Christian education. I remember as if it were yesterday, sitting under a table draped with a blanket eating dates and drinking goat's milk and being Deborah the judge. That was the beginning!

Contents

Acknowledgments ix

Introduction: Remembering God's Story xi

1. Epiphany 1
2. Martin Luther King Jr. Day 5
3. Valentine's Day 9
4. Mardi Gras 13
5. Ash Wednesday 17
6. St. Patrick's Day 21
7. Maundy Thursday 25
8. Volunteer Celebration 29
9. Earth Day 32
10. Mother's Day 36
11. Peacemaking 40
12. Pentecost 44
13. Father's Day 47
14. Juneteenth 51
15. Independence Day 55
16. Arts Festival 59
17. Evening Vacation Bible School:
    Dr. Seuss and Friends 63
18. Knit Together: Team Unity 69
19. Back to School Celebration 72
20. Labor Day 76
21. Grandparents Day 79
22. Homecoming Rally 83
23. Breads of the World Celebration 87
24. Bright Night Festival 90
25. Dia de los Muertos 93
26. Spiritual Gifts 97
27. True Thanksgiving 102
28. Las Posadas 107
29. Kwanzaa 112
30. First Night 116

Acknowledgments

I wish to thank the following people:

Laurie Ulrich, who taught me that teaching God's Word meant that you have to learn it, love it, and live it if you're going to pass it on.

The First Presbyterian Church of Homewood, St. Paul Community Church, and Flossmoor Community Church VBS planning teams from the 1970s and 1990s. I don't know who learned more—the kids or the adults. Thank you!

My editor, Rebecca Irwin-Diehl, and the editorial team at Judson for trusting me with this project.

My kids, Alex, Kailie, and Max. I want God's story to be your story, now and for all generations.

Introduction
Remembering God's Story

O my people, hear my teaching;
    listen to the words of my mouth.
I will open my mouth in parables,
    I will utter hidden things, things from of old—
what we have heard and known,
    what our fathers have told us.
We will not hide them from their children;
    we will tell the next generation
the praiseworthy deeds of the LORD,
    his power, and the wonders he has done.
He decreed statutes for Jacob
    and established the law in Israel,
which he commanded our forefathers
    to teach their children,
so the next generation would know them,
    even the children yet to be born,
    and they in turn would tell their children.
Then they would put their trust in God
    and would not forget his deeds
    but would keep his commands.
They would not be like their forefathers—
    a stubborn and rebellious generation,
whose hearts were not loyal to God,
    whose spirits were not faithful to him.
                —Psalm 78:1-8 NIV

New Life Church, where my family and I are members, is very different from the church in which I grew up and where I later worked. New Life has a membership of about 750 and counting. The membership of my home church when I was a kid was probably around 450; when I worked there as director of Christian education in the 1990s, it was down by a hundred or so. At New Life, it is not unusual for a children's ministry family event to draw three to four hundred people, the total membership of my childhood church when I was working there!

When it comes to size, my childhood church is not alone. The National Congregations Study (http://www.soc.duke.edu/natcong/index.html) conducted in 1998 and updated in 2006/2007 revealed that 56 percent of American churches have 500 or fewer regular attendees, including children; 23 percent of American churches have between 100 and 249 regular attendees, including children. The primary question I found myself facing in the 1990s is the same one that more than half of American churches are wrestling with now: *How do we build congregational community and address faith education needs for the whole church with shrinking age-grouped class sizes and volunteer pools?* Yet the deeper foundational question buried under immediate surface-level needs echoes the words of Psalm 78: *How do we continue God's story and pass it on to the next generation and the next and the next so that even our as-yet unborn children will be assured of being active participants in God's collective story, our story?*

The answers, I think, lie in returning to our roots. From the moment God created people, God also gave us families as the basic social structure of our lives. For good or bad, our first learning as children comes from those who raise us—our parents and our parents' parents, our siblings, aunts, uncles, and close family friends, all sharing knowledge and skills across generations. Scripture also calls us God's children, brothers and sisters of Christ, adopted members of the family of God. What better way to learn faith than to put God's story in the framework of shared family history and see the story come alive again and again, just as our Bible ancestors did!

Sharing God's Story

Deuteronomy 6:4-9 is called the *Shema (shay'-mah)*, or "the hear," in Judaism. I believe it provides the model for intergenerational programming. Filled with action words, the Shema gave God's people strategies for learning his word, strategies we can continue to utilize thousands of years later. God's story is the same, and the end goal is the same: connecting us to God. Why not draw on that same active learning paradigm that our Master Teacher created?

> "*Hear,* O Israel: The LORD is our God, the LORD alone. You shall *love* the LORD your God with all your heart, and with all your soul, and with all your might. *Keep* these words that I am commanding you today in your heart. *Recite* them to your children and *talk* about them when you are at home and when you are away, when you lie down and when you rise. *Bind* them as a sign on your hand, *fix* them as an emblem on your forehead, and *write* them on the doorposts of your house and on your gates." (NRSV, emphasis added)

Hear. Love. Keep. Recite. Talk. Bind. Fix. Write. Action! And action is at the heart of experiential education, which forms the framework for the intergenerational programs in this book. Experiential education is a teaching method and philosophy that involves learners in direct experience and intentional reflection in order to increase comprehension and understanding, develop skills, and shape values (The Association for Experiential Education, www.aee.org). There's an old Chinese proverb which says, "Tell me and I'll forget; show me and I may remember; involve me and I'll understand." That's experiential education in a nutshell, and that's what this book's intergenerational programs seek to do . . . actively involve learners of all ages in connecting with the Word of God. Imagine how transformed the world would be if churches could teach God's people in a holistic and relevant manner so that they would continue to increase their knowledge of God, develop skills for living from a biblical worldview, and shape their values according to God's Word. Amen. Let it be! The goal, therefore, of the intergenerational programming in this book is that it will provide opportunities for such transformational experiences. Consider now the following benefits of intergenerational programming.

There's Something for Everyone

The intergenerational programming in this book reaches out to all learners by incorporating insights from Dr. Howard Gardner's theory of multiple intelligences. Very simply put, Dr. Gardner's research observes that there are seven intelligences:

1. linguistic-verbal (learning through words)
2. logical-mathematical (learning through numbers and patterns)
3. visual-spatial (learning through shapes and graphic concepts)
4. bodily-kinesthetic (learning through using one's body and hands)
5. musical (learning through music and musical patterns)
6. interpersonal-relational (learning through interacting with others)
7. intrapersonal-introspective (learning through self-awareness or self-knowledge)

These intelligences are present in all of us in varying degrees. None works alone; rather, they work in harmony with one another. However, Gardener says that each individual will prefer one or more intelligences over the other. For educators, the application is that different learners need different teaching approaches to fully connect with the material. Some learners learn best by seeing, reading, and writing. Others need to move around and get their hands on the subject matter. Still others learn best when the content is connected to music or involves drawing or creating.

While any program's content and instructional method will not connect with every single learner all of the time, the Faith Education Station Rotation model in this book maximizes diverse learning opportunities. Hands-on experiences use a variety of approaches and techniques, so that the subject matter is explored in multiple ways in multiple settings, benefitting all of the learners some of the time, i.e. there's something for everyone.

Note: While some people may not appear to participate actively in every activity, don't count them out. Sometimes the quietest listener is the deepest thinker who may be providing support for the learning process in other ways and who will share his or her knowledge in smaller group settings or in the other situations where he or she feels more comfortable.

From Generation to Generation

Secondly, the intergenerational programming in this book allows for the exchange of knowledge across generations. Situations that mix older adults who have lots of life experience and perspective with youth who have fresh vision and new questions offer major faith development potential for all learners. In particular, youth will often ask questions that adults are too afraid to raise, yet the learning that happens because of those questions is invaluable for all ages.

Case in point: one time early on in my tenure as director of Christian education when I was telling the story of the birth of the church, a child interrupted me and asked, "So was Jesus a Christian?"

"Well, of course he was," was the answer that was about to roll off my tongue when I realized that was not accurate. Jesus was Jewish, but we're Christian. Okay, how does that work? Apparently no one had covered that particular topic in all my years of Sunday school and youth group, or maybe I'd been taking a nap when the subject had been addressed. I desperately glanced around at the other adult leaders in the room; they looked as confused as I felt.

"You know what, I'm not exactly sure how to answer that question," I told my inquisitive student. "Let me research that and get back to you next week." And so I did my homework and reported back, a little humbler and a little wiser. Just because adults are older doesn't always mean we know it all. Sometimes we have the most to learn, so why not put us in with the people who will ask the best and brightest questions without reservation—our children? The wonderful thing about intergenerational programming is that it allows for mentoring and discipling across generations. The planning team for each intergenerational event should be intentional about maximizing opportunities for community building across age groups. When dividing groups for the station rotations, mix older adults and singles in with family groups. In specific activities, facilitators can continue to pair individual families with singles and older adults so that the former has extra sets of eyes, ears, and hands and the latter feels connected and useful within the family of God. Family groups may also be split and regrouped with singles and older adults as needed.

Chameleon Christian Education

Last but not least, intergenerational ministry can encompass much more than actual events and programs. This resource book deals strictly with programs that can be run as individual events outside of the normal Sunday school time. However, don't let that stop you from adapting these lessons for your intergenerational Sunday school hour (see suggestions on page xv) or starting up an intergenerational ministry with new-mom to grand-mom mentoring pairs or an all-ages mission project. Trust that when you purposefully provide opportunities to share God's story (which is our story) across age groups, God will be at work transforming lives, from the youngest learner to the oldest. The chameleon may be a different color, but he's still a chameleon!

While these programs were created for the smaller church setting, that does not mean larger churches can't do intergenerational ministry. They certainly can and do! Churches anticipating crowds of more than 150 might consider other scheduling options, such as:

- a common fellowship time with an early and late station rotation; create a worship component on either side and provide advance sign-up for the desired time slot

- a second set of all three stations running simultaneously to accommodate a larger number of participants (assuming your facility has the space to do this)

- the full program offered on two different days or an afternoon and evening time option with advance registration.

The Format

Church Programs and Celebrations for All Generations uses what I call the Faith Education Station Rotation plan, which is similar to the Workshop Rotation Model of Christian education. (For more information on the Workshop Rotation Model, visit http://www.childrensministries.org.) Each program in

this book includes a time of worship, a time of faith development and a time of fellowship. The time of faith development involves the entire larger group being divided into three smaller groups, which then rotate through three stations. The station activities relate to the overall theme of the event yet approach the content differently, appealing to different learning styles and intelligences, and connecting the participants through experiential learning. A station host is present in each station, serving either as the storyteller or the facilitator for that activity. A planning team should be in place to handle the overall organization, publicity, registration, and facilitation of the program with additional volunteers recruited as needed.

Most programs also include a "Next Step" action to engage participants in putting their new knowledge to work. A Next Step is simply one new action that a person of any age can commit to taking to deepen his or her friendship with the Lord.

A sample intergenerational event schedule might look like this:

Registration and gathering time (15 minutes)

Opening worship (15 minutes)

Station rotations (3 stations stops of 30 minutes each with 5 minutes for making group transitions between stations) (1 hour, 45 minutes)

Meal and fellowship time (1 hour, 15 minutes)

When it comes to scheduling, do what works for your congregation. Additional songs or a short meditation can always be added to your time of worship. Fellowship time may be shortened if you are serving only refreshments and not a full meal. On matters of menu, if your church is on a tight budget, the planning team may wish to charge a small fee per household for the meal and any needed supplies (paper products, plasticware, etc.). Alternatively, consider having potluck suppers, which work best with an advance sign-up for participants.

You will notice that some programs in this book start immediately with the station rotations and end with worship followed by fellowship. The provided order is suggested, but readers should feel free to adapt the programs so that they meet your congregation's needs. I do highly recommend building in a "Gathering Time" at the beginning of the event, opening the doors and providing space and time (roughly 15 minutes) before the official start of the program, to give all participants a chance to arrive so that you can begin the event together. The planning team might provide theme-related board games or art supplies to keep the on-time arrivals busy.

The Intergenerational Toolbox

Intergenerational programming is fun. It is faith-based and builds community. It is also hard work. As in any ministry, the event planning team must take seriously the need to find a crew of volunteers and plug those volunteers into the right spots, based on their gifts and abilities. In addition, the planning team must be intentional about maximizing fellowship and learning opportunities across generations. They need to be purposeful about mixing up the whole group so that smaller groups represent the church family, not just a single demographic. The following is a list of useful "tools" for running effective intergenerational programs:

- *Space to move.* The station rotations will require three separate areas, one per station. Some stations need a large play area. The more you can spread out and get people up and moving, the better.

- *A storytelling room or storytelling box.* A space decorated with props to reflect a Bible landscape or scene. It may be a room set apart for the storytelling station or may just feature the storytelling box, which is a low, rectangular tub approximately 2' x 3' x 6". When filled with sand, the tub becomes the backdrop for stories told with small figures and props. (See programs for full details.)

- *Bible-time costumes.* Robes, tunics, headdresses, and belts that tie for both the storyteller and the participants.

- *Art supplies.* Although most of these programs can be run without many additional supplies, you will need a basic stock of art supplies, such as crayons, markers, construction paper, glue, fabric and fabric trim, craft paint, watercolors, paintbrushes, etc. Art is a frequent component of the stations.

- *Large writing surface for group responses.* Mural paper is great for participants to respond to content

with words or drawings. Provide newsprint or a whiteboard for station hosts to write down answers from brainstorming sessions.

- *Children's picture books.* Both fiction and nonfiction children's picture books are a great way to translate themed content to lifelong learning for people of all ages. Many so-called children's stories appeal to all ages. Nonfiction picture books are also wonderful resources for topics that might be difficult for a station host to explain without prior knowledge.

- *Family-friendly DVDs.* Animated classics such as Dr. Seuss and VeggieTales DVDs and films such as *Glory Road, Remember the Titans,* and *Pride* can be used to address difficult themes with most ages.

- *Behind-the-scenes volunteers.* Have people sign up in advance to handle essential tasks, such as setup, take-down, food prep, and kitchen cleanup, so that the program runs smoothly.

- *Worship leader.* Also in advance, recruit someone to handle all music needs, whether in worship or in a station.

- *Station hosts.* These may be regular volunteers or "experts" recruited to match their gifts and talents with their station activities where possible. Because station hosts often double as storytellers (see below), place these volunteers carefully. Also ensure that station hosts and storytellers alike are capable of communicating ideas to children as well as to adults and avoid complex explanations or big theological or technical words.

- *Storytellers.* Seek out volunteers who have natural dramatic flair and a willingness to "get into character" for each particular Bible story. Most stories are best told in first person, so the storyteller will be bringing the Bible character to life. Give the storyteller the biblical story text at least a month in advance, including any helpful background or contextual information. The more comfortable and familiar the storyteller is with the story, the easier it will be to communicate the character's joys, concerns, problems, fears, etc., in first person. Encourage storytellers to involve the participants in the story by having them mime additional character roles.

Continuing God's Story

While each chapter in *Church Programs and Celebrations for All Generations* is set up for an extended three- to four-hour event, the individual stations can be adapted for use on a weekly basis in a Workshop Rotation Model in Sunday school classes or other existing settings. Your Christian education team would simply need to add a fourth station to round out a month of activities.

If your church adapts one of the programs in *Church Programs and Celebrations for All Generations* or if you have a success story you'd like to share and other tips or resources to pass along, please visit this book's website at www.forallgenerations.com and let Rachel know. We'll post your stories on the website with your contact information as a way of equipping and encouraging one another as we "tell the next generation the praiseworthy deeds of the LORD, his power, and the wonders he has done" so that all of God's children "would put their trust in God and would not forget his deeds but would keep his commands" (Psalm 78:4, 7 NIV).

CHAPTER 1

January
Epiphany

Leader Background

It was probably from the example of the magi, who brought Jesus gifts of gold and the precious perfumes of frankincense and myrrh, that Christians began to give presents as part of their Christmas celebrations. For most people in the U.S., that tradition has shifted and become associated primarily with Christmas Eve and Christmas Day, but in other cultures, the primary day for gift-giving is January 6, often called Three Kings Day or the Feast of Epiphany.

Epiphany around the World

The Feast of Epiphany (also known as the Adoration of the Magi) marks the end of the twelve days of Christmas. It commemorates primarily the visit of the three wise men to the home of the Christ child. In the United States, some people "celebrate" it by taking down their Christmas trees, nativity scenes, and other decorations. In many countries around the world, Three Kings Day is celebrated as a holiday itself, with carols and songs, special traditional foods, and the exchange of gifts or treats for the children. For example, in Belgium and the Netherlands, children go "caroling" in groups of three and receive coins or treats in exchange for their musical gift. In France, people bake *gâteau des Rois* (king cakes) and hide a small figurine or bean inside. Whoever bites the piece of cake with the "king" in it gets to be ruler for the day! In Puerto Rico, the Philippines, and parts of Mexico and Latin America, children leave shoes or boxes lined with straw for the three kings (not Santa Claus) to fill with treats.

Program Focus: Visit of the three magi or wise men to the Christ child

Key Verse: "When they saw that the star had stopped, they were overwhelmed with joy" (Matthew 2:10 NRSV).

Purpose:
a. To highlight the biblical basis for Epiphany and why we celebrate it
b. To explore the idea of gifts we bring to Jesus
c. To give thanks for and celebrate Jesus' birth

Epiphany in the Bible

The biblical story of the wise men's visit can be found only in Matthew 2. Take time to read it and familiarize yourself with the events and how they fit into the Christmas story. Did you know that the three kings didn't actually show up at the manger in Bethlehem on the heels of the shepherds? They probably arrived a year or two later. Bible scholars do not have a set date, but since the star appeared on the night of Jesus' birth, it would have taken some time for the kings to travel from their homeland—most likely modern-day Iran—to Israel.

Did you also notice that these men weren't kings in the sense of being royal rulers? The Bible calls them magi or wise men, meaning they were scholars who studied the stars and the ancient prophecies—a cross between our modern astronomers and astrologers. These learned scholars knew the prophecies laid out in the Old Testament book of Isaiah. They came from the east, following a newborn star, and they came with the sole purpose of worshiping the child who was prophesied to be the Messiah, the anointed king of the Jews. They set out on a mission to find this special, long-awaited child, bearing precious gifts for the infant king, following yonder star, and not giving up until they found him. What a journey! What devotion! Do we share the same commitment?

Worship

Opening Song(s): "We Three Kings of Orient Are," "What Child Is This," "Crown Him with Many Crowns," "All Hail the Power of Jesus' Name"

Call to Worship:

Leader: We come today, seeking the King.

People: The baby born to be King of the Jews.

Leader: We've traveled far, for more than a year.

People: To find the baby born to be King of the Jews.

Leader: May we find this infant King and worship him.

People: Glory to God in the highest, and on earth, peace, goodwill to all.

Scripture Reading: Matthew 2:1-12

Sung Response: "Open the Eyes of My Heart" (Sonic Flood) or "Be Thou My Vision," "Majesty, Worship His Majesty," "Let All Mortal Flesh Keep Silent"

Time of Prayer: Pray for this evening's program, that God will be present, that hearts and minds will be open to learning more about him, for any prayer concerns, etc.

Closing Song: "Shout to the Lord," "Praise Him, Praise Him," "As with Gladness Men of Old"

Faith Stations

Station 1. Where in the World Are the Three Magi?

What You'll Need

Volunteers: station host

World globe

Large wall map of the Middle East today

Smaller map of the Middle East, photocopied for each person

Star stickers

Books on astrology and dream interpretation

Bibles with sticky notes marking the books of the Prophets

Large star (handmade from cardboard or something fancier)

Jesus and his cradle/crib (Use a doll's bed or create your own using a cardboard box lined with a blanket; place a large doll, perhaps sitting up, inside.)

Gold, frankincense, and myrrh (Three kings gift sets can be ordered online for approximately $30, or you can create your own. *Note:* Frankincense and myrrh are usually represented as large bottles of fragrant oil or perfume.)

Ahead of time, set up this station so that participants will move in a path as they discover more about the magi. If possible, identify a second door where participants may exit as they complete the path. The station host should welcome participants to the station and explain the five areas they will visit within the room. Then the host may either act as a guide to lead participants around the area or provide written instructions at each stop.

Stop 1. Feature the globe. Invite participants to locate their home country, as well as the Middle East (Israel and Iran).

Stop 2. Post the large wall map and provide photocopies of the smaller map. Point out Iran (formerly Persia, thought to be home of the magi) and Israel (homeland of Jesus) on the large map. Distribute star stickers and the photocopies so participants can mark on their individual maps the locations of Tehran, Iran, and Bethlehem, Israel, and then draw a line connecting the two cities. If time allows, ask if anyone can estimate the distance between them (nearly 1,000 miles).

Stop 3. Have a table holding books on astrology and dream interpretation and Bibles marked with the books of the Prophets. Ask participants to read Isaiah 9:1-7 aloud in their small group. Explain that the magi would have been familiar with these prophetic words. They were looking for this child who would become Wonderful Counselor, Mighty God, Everlasting Father, Prince of Peace who descended from the throne of King David. The wise men consulted the stars (comparable to modern-day astrology) and interpreted dreams, but they also knew the words of the Old Testament prophets very well. These words sent them on their quest to find the baby Jesus.

Stop 4. Hang the star and arrange Jesus' cradle and the gifts of the magi. Invite participants to stand or kneel as they are able and say a quiet prayer, personally thanking God for giving us the example of the three magi who never gave up their search for the infant King, Jesus. Allow people to put a dab of frankincense and myrrh oil on their hand, forehead, arm, or even on their map to take home with them. Encourage children especially to touch and hold the gift of gold.

Stop 5. Post the text of Matthew 2:10 on newsprint or a whiteboard, and provide participants with writing implements so they can copy the key verse on their map.

At the end of the rotation, ask the group to leave by a different doorway (if possible) or send them to their next station via a different route through the church. Explain that this symbolizes the alternative path the magi took home after an angel warned them in a dream to avoid King Herod, who wanted information about Jesus, the prophesied king.

Station 2. Give a Gift of . . .

What You'll Need

Volunteers: station host
Writing implements (pens, pencils, crayons)
Large banner that reads "Give the Gift of Yourself!" (use an 8' sheet of mural paper with a star drawn at the top; depending on the number of participants, you may need to provide one banner for each small group)
12" cardboard people forms (handmade or order from art or school supply company)
Markers, crayons
Glue sticks
Scissors (including safety scissors for children's use)
Various gift decorations (wrapping paper, ribbon, bows, gift tags)
Old magazines, catalogs, and greeting cards

Ahead of time, hang the banner on the wall, and put the cardboard people and various art supplies on a table(s) in the station area. As participants arrive, the station host should welcome the group and ask people to sit at the worktables. Invite participants to think about their own skills, talents, or favorite activities; then instruct everyone to look for pictures that represent these God-given gifts and interests. These pictures will be glued onto a cardboard person. If time allows, participants may also decorate the person to look like themselves.

When participants are finished decorating their cardboard people, ask for a few individuals to describe the gifts depicted on their people. Explain that these are all gifts that we can give back to Jesus. God has given us these gifts. Our job is to use them to glorify him and in service to him. When we love and serve in Jesus' name, we are giving God the gift of ourselves. Ask the table groups to explain their people to each other.

After this time of group sharing, invite each person to wrap up his or her person like a present and add a gift tag that says: "To Jesus, From [insert name]." The wrapped gifts can be attached to the banner.

Close in prayer, giving thanks for the gifts God has given, not only in the birth of Jesus, but in the form of talents and passions that people can use in service to God. Ask God to continue to equip and encourage participants to serve in Jesus' name.

At the close of the event, hang the gift-laden banner(s) prominently in the church where all worshipers can see it. After two weeks, invite participants to remove their personal gifts and take them home, where the package(s) may be unwrapped and hung to remind them of the gifts they can give to Jesus each and every day.

Station 3. Celebration Time

What You'll Need

Volunteers: station host

Construction paper (12" x 18" sheets, cut in half)

Newspaper or plastic covers to protect tabletops

Assorted stickers

Markers and crayons

Glitter glue, watercolor paintbrushes, and small plates (squeeze moderate amount of glue onto plate and use brush to apply)

Index cards

Tape or staplers

Pinking shears or scrapbook scissors and punches; safety scissors for children's use

In advance, set up tables and chairs, cover the tables with newspaper or plastic covers, and set out sufficient art supplies. As participants arrive, the station host should welcome them with an invitation to sit at the worktables. Explain that in this station, each person will make a crown to wear to symbolize the Magi who searched for Jesus, a fellow king.

Provide the following instructions, either in writing at each table or verbally to the entire group.

Create a Crown

1. Tape or staple together one end of two 6" x 18" strips of construction paper (precut).

2. Size the crown according to each person's head and cut the strip to size. (A little long is better, so that you can easily staple or tape it closed after decorating.)

3. Cut the top edge of the length of paper to make a crown shape, using decorative-edge scissors, or simply cut a row of 3"–4" Vs along the top edge.

4. Decorate the crown with glitter glue, stickers, markers, and crayons.

5. After allowing a little time for the glue to dry, tape or staple the ends of the strip together to form a crown.

When crowns are finished, distribute index cards and invite participants to write an Epiphany poem for Jesus to be read at the party at the end of the program. A simple poem form, especially for children, is the acrostic. Write the letters of Jesus' name along the left edge of the index card, with one letter per line. For each letter, think of a word or phrase beginning with that letter that describes or celebrates Jesus.

The host can close this session with prayer, thanking God for the gift of Jesus and repeating the key verse: "When they saw that the star had stopped, they were overwhelmed with joy" (Matthew 2:10 NRSV).

Fellowship

It works well to have your fellowship time at the end of this Epiphany event. However, this event can be tailored to your group's needs and time constraints. Just be sure to include a time of fellowship in your program, and to serve refreshments with a star-shaped theme. Provide star-shaped cookies or a cake decorated with candy or icing stars. Invite participants to wear their crowns like party hats and to read their poems in honor of the infant King. Consider closing the event with a benediction in the form of the final stanza of Christina Rosetti's poem, "In the Bleak Midwinter," or sing the hymn by the same name (1872).

> What can I give Him, poor as I am?
> If I were a shepherd, I would bring a lamb;
> If I were a wise man, I would do my part;
> Yet what I can I give Him: Give my heart.

CHAPTER 2

January
Martin Luther King Jr. Day

Leader Background

Martin Luther King Jr. was born and raised in Atlanta, Georgia. The son of a minister, M.L. (as he was called as a child) grew up influenced by his father's words, which followed from the Bible. Dr. King himself became a minister too, and worked to encourage and support those who were fighting for peace and equal rights. He was assassinated in 1966 while in Memphis, Tennessee, where he was supporting striking sanitation workers. Because of Dr. King's belief in nonviolence and his passion for healing the brokenness in this world, many parallels may be drawn between his life and the life and ministry of Jesus, parallels that will be explored through this event. In addition, in 1994 Congress designated the Martin Luther King Jr. federal holiday as a national day of service, which align with Jesus' words that he came not to be served but to serve. An extension activity in this program offers participants the opportunity to explore a group "next step" of planning a day of service in honor of MLK and our King, Jesus. See http://www.mlkday.gov/about/overview/index.asp for more information.

Note: another way to run this program would be to invite members of an immigrant community or a culturally distinct sister congregation to participate in this event with you. Your planning team should be sure to communicate well with the contact people for your invited group, in addition to being intentional about mixing home church and visiting group participants in the station rotations. During fellowship time, your planning team may also want to play some group games/mixers to further connect people.

Program Focus: Martin Luther King Jr.; following God's will to seek righteousness

Key Verse: "'Blessed are those who are persecuted for righteousness' sake, for theirs is the kingdom of heaven'" (Matthew 5:10 NRSV).

Purpose:
a. To explore Martin Luther King Jr. as a seeker of righteousness who was responding to God's call to serve
b. To explore parallels between Jesus and Martin Luther King Jr.
c. To identify examples of injustice in this world and plan a "next step" for seeking righteousness

Worship

Opening Song(s): Choose 3–5 songs that support the theme of righteousness, peacemaking, and social justice. Possibilities include "We Shall Overcome," "Mine Eyes Have Seen the Glory," "This Little Light of Mine," "Let There Be Peace on Earth."

Scripture Reading: Matthew 5:1-12 (the Beatitudes)

Time of Prayer: Take personal prayer requests from participants or ask them to name specific instances of social injustice for which they would like to pray. Ahead of time the planning team can also search "Martin Luther King Day prayers" on the Internet and find a variety of prayers and litanies already written by various church denominations and organizations to remember this man and mark this day.

Faith Stations

Station 1. Who Was MLK?

What You'll Need

Volunteer: station host

Assortment of MLK picture book biographies from your library (see also
http://www.kinderkorner.com/mlk.html for title suggestions)

Martin's Big Words by Doreen Rappaport (Jump at the Sun/Hyperion Books, 2001)

Assortment of chairs and tables or couches, big pillows, and blankets (optional)

Ahead of time, set up this station as a reading room. If you have a room available with couches and comfortable chairs, use that space. If you don't have a gathering area like that, choose a room where you can create a story circle by setting out blankets or big floor pillows for participants or by arranging smaller circles of chairs. Distribute picture book biographies on MLK around the space. You should have plenty to choose from. Ask your local library to help you find as many copies as you can for your event.

The station host should welcome participants and invite them to gather in a semicircle. Read aloud *Martin's Big Words* (or another illustrated biography of

your choosing) to the group. After the story, ask participants to form smaller groups of 3–5 people and discuss the following questions:

1. What did you already know about Dr. King before you heard the story?

2. What is one thing you admire about Dr. King?

3. What is one goal or dream that Jesus and Dr. King seem to have in common?

As time allows after the discussion, the host may invite people to look through the different picture books around the room and read another one or two in their own story circle.

Station 2. Powerful Words

What You'll Need

Volunteer: station host

Photocopies of MLK quotes (search the Internet for "MLK quotes")

White card stock or copy paper

Cardboard and glue (optional)

Pencils, pens, crayons, thin markers

Bibles bookmarked for Matthew 5:1-12 and 22:37-39

Concordances

2 sheets of mural paper (approximately 4' x 10'–12')

Wide-tipped markers

Photocopies of MLK speeches (see www.mlkonline.net)

Adult business attire, including suit jackets, shirts and blouses, neckties and scarves

Podium (or something to distinguish a speaker)

Before the event, set up the room with three distinct areas as outlined below. Participants will rotate through the three stops in Station 2 as prompted by the station host.

Stop 1. Arrange tables and chairs; distribute photocopies of MLK quotes, pens, pencils, crayons, thin markers, cardboard and glue (optional), Bibles, and concordances

Stop 2. Hang mural paper and provide several wide-tipped markers

Stop 3. Set up podium; provide photocopies of MLK speeches and business attire for dress-up

The station host should welcome participants to this station and explain that Dr. King used powerful words to move hearts to action. He used words to encourage. He used words to teach. He used words to heal. He used words to motivate. He used words to tell the truth. This station offers several different ways to experience Dr. King's words.

Invite participants to start with Stop 1 to review the actual words of MLK and Jesus. Then they can contribute to the 2 mural sheets at Stop 2 or the role play at Stop 3. The host should circulate throughout the room, helping as needed.

Stop 1. Instruct each family (or each member in the family group) to choose a favorite MLK quote from the provided photocopies and a related quote from Jesus in Scripture. (The Matthew passages are rich with verses that complement Dr. King's teachings, or participants may use the concordances to find alternative verses.) Participants should copy both quotes onto the white paper or card stock.

As time allows, participants may decorate the paper's edge to frame their quotes. Supply glue and cardboard for backing if you expect participants to prefer a sturdier craft. (If participants have already been to the It's Not Fair station, they can attach their "next step" card to the back of their favorite quotes page.)

Stop 2. At this stop, the host should write "MLK" at the top of the first sheet of mural paper and "Jesus" at the top of the second. Then invite participants to use the wide-tipped markers and mural paper to create two lists—one comprised of words that describe Dr. King and the things he did to seek peace, justice, and healing for all people, and the second doing the same for Jesus. They can also compare their quote sheets from Stop 1 and share what they learned about MLK in other stations.

Stop 3. Here the host will invite participants to dress up and stand at the podium (or some equivalent) to read excerpts of MLK's speeches out loud to their fellow group members. Be sure to encourage school-aged children as well as adults to take the podium. Remind participants to have fun with the dramatic elements of this stop!

Station 3. It's Not Fair

What You'll Need

Volunteer: station host

Index cards (3" x 5")

Pens and pencils

2 bowls

Transparent tape

Chairs and tables

The station host should welcome family groups and ask them to sit in small conversation circles. Distribute a supply of index cards and writing implements to each circle.

Explain that Dr. King worked to make life fair for everyone. He also wanted to teach people that when life wasn't fair, they shouldn't give up or do bad things to get their way. They should continue to follow God's teachings to work for peace and righteousness, mercy and love. Still, the host may acknowledge, it is a very human reaction to cry out, "But it's not fair!"

Encourage each group to think of situations in their own life experiences and in the larger world that make them cry out, "It's not fair!" Then invite them to write down (or draw a picture of) each of these unfair things on the index cards. While adults may focus on issues of racial injustice or unfair treatment on the job, small children are more likely to volunteer statements such as, "When my brother gets a new toy and I don't" or "When my sister gets to lick the cookie batter bowl and I don't." That's okay. Encourage all participants to contribute because all of us, from small children to older adults, know the feeling of "It's not fair!"

After about 10 minutes of brainstorming and writing, ask participants to read their cards out loud. Then identify whether the unfairness issue is personal (applying to a specific individual) or global (affecting a large group of people), and make two piles of cards accordingly.

After reviewing the cards, encourage each individual to choose a personal "next step" in fighting unfairness and write down that action plan on a new index card. For example, the child offended by a sibling's new toy might decide, "I will not fight with my brother over the new toy; instead, I will be happy for him and ask nicely if I can play with him." The adult concerned about racial prejudice against immigrants in her community might resolve, "I will contact my church's social justice ministry team and ask how I can get involved in being an advocate for 'strangers' in our land."

After the group has also participated in Station 2: Powerful Words, participants may tape their "next steps" card to the back of their favorite quotes paper.

Extension activity: During this rotation, the host can ask the groups to choose a "next step" service project that would send the participants out into the community and/or connect them with a culturally distinct sister congregation or immigrant group in the area. Your planning team may want to research some options for the host to present to get people thinking. If a guest group has joined you for the event, this would be a great time to get all participants thinking about joint service opportunities.

Station 4: "I Have a Dream" Video (optional)

Depending on the age of your participants (this would work better for a group of school-aged and older participants), you might add a fourth station to your rotation or include this video during your Sunday worship service. Dr. King's "I Have a Dream"

speech is available on multiple video websites, including YouTube.com and mlkonline.net. It is also downloadable from video.google.com. Just do an Internet search for "MLK I Have a Dream video download" and choose the option that works best for you.

After viewing the video as a larger group, you could break into small conversation circles for discussion. Questions might include:

- How does this speech make you feel?
- How does Dr. King remind you of Jesus?
- If Dr. King were alive today, do you think he'd say the same thing? Why or why not?
- If not, what might he say instead?
- In what ways do you share Dr. King's dream?
- What are two things you can do personally to help keep Dr. King's dream alive?

Close your discussion time in prayer.

Fellowship

Your planning team will need to decide how you want your event to flow. Do you want to start with a meal, then go to the faith stations, and close with worship? Or do you want to open with worship, go to the faith stations, and end with punch and cookies? If you've invited a guest group to participate in this event, think about serving a multicultural potluck banquet at the beginning or end of the program or do research online to find examples of MLK's favorite foods and serve those (pecan pie seems to be a recurring theme). In any case, your event can be tailored to your group's needs and time constraints. Just be sure to include a time of fellowship in your program, whether a full meal or light refreshments.

January | Chinese New Year

Invite Chinese, Korean, or Vietnamese Americans to be special guests or guest station hosts at an Asian New Year celebration (which falls variously between January 20 and February 20). Set up three stations that help participants explore the guests' culture, such as making dragons and lions for a New Year parade, preparing egg rolls or spring rolls, and listening to an invited guest tell a favorite Bible story in his or her language. When possible work with members of the actual cultures to plan activities. (See www.forallgenerations.com for more program ideas.)

CHAPTER 3

February
Valentine's Day

Leader Background

Valentine's Day is a secular holiday with roots in both Christian and pagan traditions. Similar to how early Christians set the date for Christmas in December to replace the pagan Roman sun festival during the darkest days of winter, Valentine's Day may have been set in February to replace the pagan Roman feast of Lupercalia, which celebrated fertility and purity. Other scholars believe the mid-February date coincided with the burial date of Saint Valentine, a church leader who either helped persecuted Christians or was persecuted himself in the early days of the church in Rome. Pope Gelasius set February 14 as Valentine's Day around AD 498. The holiday has been celebrated since then, with Americans first exchanging Valentine's Day greetings in the 1700s. The first mass-produced valentines made of ribbon, lace, and pretty pictures were created and sold by Esther A. Howland in the 1840s.

Worship

Opening Song(s): Open your time together with 3–5 songs of praise and worship that support the theme of love—both God's love for us and our love for God. Possibilities include "Jesus Loves Me," "Love Divine, All Loves Excelling," "Hallelujah, Your Love Is Amazing," "I Could Sing of Your Love Forever."

Scripture Reading: 1 John 4:7-13

Time of Prayer: Take general prayer requests or ask people to share prayer concerns for friends and family members who need to feel God's love right now. Depending on the size of your group, the leader could open prayer time and then go around the room asking each person to say the first name of the person in need of God's love.

Closing Song: "They Will Know We Are Christians by Our Love"

Program Focus: Love your neighbor

Key Verse: "'Love one another as I have loved you'" (John 15:12 NRSV).

Purpose:
a. To introduce a biblical base to a secular holiday through the use of John 15:12
b. To identify examples of how Jesus loved others
c. To make a personal "next step" that will model God's love to another person

Faith Stations

Note: In this program, groups will go only to Stations 1 and 2 during the first hour. After participants have visited both 1 and 2, they can all move to Station 3, so make sure you have enough space for all participants to do the closing activity.

Station 1. Loving Like Jesus

What You'll Need

Volunteers: station host, someone to run camera (optional)

Bibles

Copies of the list of Jesus love stories (Mark 10:46-52; John 9:1-11; Luke 5:17-25; Luke 6:27-36; Luke 7:36-50; Luke 15:3-10; Luke 15:11-32)

Bible-time costumes (robes, ties, head coverings, walking staffs, etc.)

Video camera, tripod, and tape (optional)

This station will get people directly involved in the love stories that made up Jesus' daily life. The host should welcome participants and gather them in a semicircle. Explain that participants will be choosing a Jesus love story and acting it out for the group. Families can split up or stay together as needed so that everyone has a chance to participate. The easiest way to do these simple dramas is to have a narrator read the passage and assign actors to pantomime the characters' actions in the passage. However, actors may also read or speak lines as desired. Briefly summarize the love stories for the group and then allow them to choose the one they want to use. It's okay if multiple groups use the same story.

The love stories are as follows: Mark 10:46-52 and John 9:1-11 (the healings of Bartimaeus and of the man born blind); Luke 5:17-25 (the paralytic lowered through the roof and healed by Jesus); Luke 6:27-36 (Jesus' command to love one another and other principles for Christian living); Luke 7:36-50 (Jesus' forgiving of the sinful woman); Luke 15:3-10 (the parables of the lost sheep and the lost coin); and Luke 15:11-32 (the parable of the prodigal son).

Give the groups 15–20 minutes to read through the passage, decide on roles, and practice a few times. They may use costumes or props as needed. Save 10–15 minutes at the end of the session for groups to perform their dramas. You may want to have a volunteer videotape the skits so that you can play them on a TV during worship or fellowship time.

Station 2. Love Story

What You'll Need

Volunteer: station host

The Giving Tree by Shel Silverstein (or other love-theme picture book of your choosing)

Bibles

The station host should welcome the group and ask them to gather in a circle for a story. Explain that the group will now hear a love story—not a romantic love story, but a story about loving one's friends above all else. This is the kind of love that Jesus has for us. First, read from John 15:9-17 and ask people to keep those words of Jesus in mind as they listen to you read *The Giving Tree*.

After the story, the group can break into smaller circles for 10–15 minutes of discussion. Questions can be printed on a flip chart or whiteboard or be distributed in a handout. Ask things like:

1. How did the tree care for the boy when he was young?

2. What did the tree do for the boy as he got older?

3. How did the tree show love for the boy even when she was very old and small?

4. Jesus tells us to love one another as he loved us. Listen to these words again from Jesus (read John 15:9-17). Do you think the tree was showing the boy Jesus-love? Why?

5. What is one way a friend or family member has shown you this kind of Jesus-love?

Note: If you choose a different story to read to your group, you will also need to come up with new discussion questions.

Station 3. Jesus Valentines

What You'll Need

Volunteer: station host

Valentine form (Draw 2 hearts on an 8½" x 11" sheet of paper. In the center of each heart, write, "Jesus said, '. . . love one another as I have loved you' [John 15:12 NRSV]. *Jesus, I promise to love you by. . . ."* Make a copy of this valentine form on pink card stock [or copy paper] for each person.)

Valentine supplies (ribbon, lace, stickers, markers, crayons, glue sticks, glitter, pens, scissors, etc.)

The station host should welcome participants to this closing activity and explain that they are going to make a valentine for Jesus. Jesus asks us to love one another as Jesus has loved us, so participants need to think of at least one way they can show this Jesus-love to someone else. Participants should cut out the heart and write on it their promise(s) to Jesus. Then they can decorate the hearts. Remind participants to put this valentine somewhere they will see it daily—tape it to the bathroom mirror or their headboard or the refrigerator. (If your budget allows, you can also provide self-stick magnets that can be placed on the back of the valentines.)

This activity can very naturally flow into fellowship time, whether this is a full meal or just dessert/snacks. Fellowship time would be a great opportunity to play back the videotaped skits or have groups perform them live. For additional structured activities to use while participants are finishing their Jesus valentines, go to www.forallgenerations.com for the "Broken Hearts" and "Valentine Tracker" activities by Elizabeth Crisci (*Celebrate Good Times*, Judson Press, 2005).

February | African American History Month

The entire month of February has been set aside in the U.S. calendar as a time for education and celebration centered on African American culture and history. For more background information and creative ideas, visit www.smithsonian education.org/educators/resource_library/african_american_resources.html.

• **African American Film Festival.** Show one movie per week. Choose family-friendly films (e.g., *Pride, Glory Road, Remember the Titans, The Long Walk Home*) and facilitate an intergenerational small-group discussion after the movie. Or, if time is an issue, show a movie one week and the next week host a program with three stations that explore the film's themes from a faith-based perspective (see sample program at www.forall generations.com). This idea is particularly good for a primarily white or multicultural congregation. Just be sure to preview the movies as a planning team and provide church members with appropriate rating and age-level advisories.

• **African American Arts Festival.** Design three stations that allow participants of all ages to experience authentic African or African American arts and crafts, including masks, a shekere rattle, and an adire cloth. In conjunction with the program, host a bazaar and sell traditional handicrafts with the proceeds benefiting a faith-based relief program in Africa. For sample craft products, visit a website such as www.brighthope .org/index.php.

• **African American Food Festival.** Offer a weekly cooking class in February featuring child-friendly recipes from Africa or from African American culture here in the United States (i.e., "soul food"). Finish off the month with a celebration in which class members prepare their favorite recipe and share it with the larger congregation in a potluck fellowship. Consider charging a nominal fee for attendees, and donate the proceeds to a youth missions project or a local ministry that benefits African American youth.

Fellowship

Ideally this program should close with a time of fellowship. Consider serving heart-shaped cookies or minicakes, strawberries and raspberries, red gelatin, strawberry sundaes, chocolate brownies or candy, or other Valentine-themed food. However, your planning team will need to decide how you want your event to flow. Do you want to start with a meal, then go to the faith stations, and close with worship? Or do you want to open with worship, go to the faith stations, and end with punch and cookies? Each event can be tailored to your group's needs and time constraints. Just be sure to include a time of fellowship in your program, whether a full meal or light refreshments.

CHAPTER 4

February
Mardi Gras

Program Focus: Celebration and sacrifice

Key Verse: "For everything there is a season, and a time for every matter under heaven" (Ecclesiastes 3:1 NRSV).

Purpose:
a. To explore the historical Christian roots of Mardi Gras and how it connects to Lent
b. To create a time of fellowship, celebrating Christian community
c. To explore the meaning of Ecclesiastes 3 and how it connects to Mardi Gras and Lent

Leader Background

Mardi Gras literally means "Fat Tuesday" and became known as a final day of no-holds-barred celebration before the solemn time of soul-searching during Lent (the 40 days before Easter, excluding Sundays). Much like Valentine's Day, the feast day of Mardi Gras emerged, over the centuries, as a way to subtly win over the pagans in Rome who, for hundreds of years, had celebrated Lupercalia, an early spring fertility festival that was finally outlawed by Pope Gelasius at the end of the fifth century AD. Gelasius replaced the celebration with the Feast of the Purification of the Virgin Mary, tying in the aspects of purification and fertility but abolishing the often lewd and lascivious traditions that had accompanied Lupercalia. As church leaders continued to battle culturally entrenched pagan rites and rituals, they slowly began to rename and reshape these non-Christian celebrations into ones with faith-based roots. Carnival (which translates to "farewell to the flesh") emerged as the period between Epiphany and Ash Wednesday, in which people binged on stored-up meat and dairy items in preparation for Lent, which required meals of fish or times of fasting. Mardi Gras, celebrated the day before Ash Wednesday, was the final all-out party of the season. When Mardi Gras traditions emigrated from Europe to America in the 1700s, Americans living in New Orleans were quick to adopt their ancestors' traditions but add their own independent touches. Mardi Gras became known as the season that stretched from Epiphany to Lent, and the day before Ash Wednesday slowly morphed into a day of decadent revelry. However, the spiritual roots of Mardi Gras lead us to remember that "for everything there is a season, and a time for every matter under heaven" (Ecclesiastes 3:1 NRSV).

Gathering Time

What You'll Need

Green, gold, and purple streamers

Balloons

Tape

Blank mask forms (cardboard or wood from a craft store or catalog)

Mask decorating supplies (glitter, sequins, markers, glue, feathers)

Mural paper

Markers for mural paper

As participants come in, ask them to help decorate your fellowship area with green, gold, and purple streamers and balloons. They can also decorate paper masks to hang on the walls. You might also want to have a big sheet of mural paper on the wall with the statement "Mardi Gras is . . ." and let participants complete the statement with words or pictures.

Note: For this program, it is best if worship follows the station rotations and comes before the fellowship time, as participants will be baking king cakes, which will need oven time.

Faith Stations

Station 1. King Cakes

What You'll Need

Volunteer: station host

King cake ingredients (hot roll mix [1 box for every 8 people], hot roll mix ingredients per package directions [eggs, hot water], white sugar, cinnamon, butter, flour)

Rolling pins

Tubs of white frosting; green, yellow, and purple food coloring or colored sugar sprinkles; a dozen or so big raisins, beans, or miniature plastic babies to hide in king cakes

Non-stick cooking spray or butter

Baking sheets

Mixing bowls

Plastic table coverings for work surface

Mixing spoons

Oven

The station host should welcome participants and explain that king cakes are a traditional Mardi Gras food. King cakes were first served on Epiphany (January 6) in honor of the three wise men who visited the Christ child. Epiphany marks the start of the Mardi Gras season. The cakes later were decorated with the Mardi Gras colors of green, gold, and purple, which represent faith, power, and justice. Inside each king cake is a tiny toy baby. This represents the Christ child. Tradition holds that whoever finds the Christ child in his or her piece of cake will host the next Mardi Gras party or provide next year's king cake. Groups will be baking king cakes to serve during fellowship time. Encourage everyone to share in this process.

The easiest way to do this project is to set up long tables right outside your church kitchen and cover them with disposable plastic table cloths. Participants should gather in groups of 6–10 people, depending on your total group size. Prepare the hot roll mix dough according to the package directions. Shape into a large ball and cover with the bowl (upside down). Let rest for 5 minutes.

Then knead dough for 5 minutes. Sprinkle flour on the work area and roll the dough out into a rectangle about 1/2" thick.

Melt a stick of butter and spoon onto your rectangle. Sprinkle the butter with white sugar and cinnamon. Then roll up the dough into a log like a jellyroll. Make sure to put the baby or one raisin in before rolling completely.

Stretch the dough lengthwise and join the ends so that the log now forms an oval. Pinch the ends together. Place on a lightly greased baking sheet. Cover with a towel and set in the kitchen to rise for 20 minutes. The station host will put the king cakes in the oven to bake at 375 degrees for 30 minutes.

Before the group rotates to the next station, they can wash their dishes and clean up their work areas.

Station 2. For Everything There Is a Season

What You'll Need

Volunteer: station host

1 make-your-own calendar packet per family group
(use your own computer software or an Internet site
template—search "make your own calendar")

Pens

Markers

Stickers

Old calendars/magazines to cut up for pictures

Glue sticks

Hole punch

Ribbon

Flip chart/whiteboard and markers

This station should be set up with long worktables. Each table should be set up with make-your-own calendar packets and supplies to share. The station host should welcome the group and ask participants to sit at the tables in their family groups. If you have singles and/or older adults who have joined with a family, keep those groups together but give one calendar packet to each head of household.

Start a discussion about how we organize our time. Use the flip chart or whiteboard to write down group answers to the following questions:

1. How many calendars do you have in your house? (family, Mom's, Dad's, work, etc.)

2. What kind of information is already printed on a calendar? (holidays/seasons)

3. What kind of information do you add to your household calendar?

4. Can you think of certain dates or seasons that would be marked on a church calendar? (Epiphany, Ash Wednesday, Lent, Holy Week, Maundy Thursday, Good Friday, Easter, Pentecost, Advent, Christmas, etc.)

Then the host should introduce the calendar-making activity by covering these points:

1. Mardi Gras became an all-out party day on the day before the beginning of Lent.

2. The Lenten season in the church is a time of reflection and prayer, of considering the power of Jesus' sacrifice for us.

3. Lent ends with Easter Sunday, which is the celebration of Jesus' rising from the dead and saving us from our sins.

4. Think about what you could sacrifice for Jesus. Many Christians give up something during the season of Lent to remind themselves of Jesus' sacrifice on the cross.

5. Some people give up sweet treats like chocolate or dessert. Others give up a time-wasting habit like watching TV or playing video games. Some people choose to go without eating one day each week, which is called fasting. All of these sacrifices are done to draw people closer to Jesus and make time to connect with him.

6. As you put together your calendar today, pay attention to the things you and your family make time for. Write down holidays, birthdays, anniversaries, and vacations. Write down church activities as well.

Then the host should ask the participants these questions:

1. Even though the days pass by and activities on our calendars change with the months or the seasons, God is always with us, day by day, month by month, season by season. Do you think you and your family make enough time for God on your calendar? Why or why not?

2. What is one thing you can do to spend more time with God?

Give families 15 minutes or so to add personal dates (birthdays, anniversaries, vacations, etc.) to the calendars and decorate each page with stickers, picture cutouts, or markers/crayons.

Station 3. Sacrifice and Celebration

What You'll Need

Volunteer: station host

A Tale of Three Trees by Angela Elwell Hunt

The station host should welcome participants to this activity and explain that they're going to hear a story about three trees who dream about what they want to be someday. Their dreams come true, but not in the way they'd imagined. They sacrifice their dreams to accept God's will for their lives. When they realize how they fit into God's master plan, it is truly a time of joyous celebration.

After reading the story, the host should ask participants to gather in groups of 6–10 people and answer the following questions:

1. What is something that would be easy for you to give up and do without?

2. What is something that would be difficult for you to give up and do without?

3. What is something that would be impossible for you to give up and do without?

4. What did God give up for you? How can you celebrate this amazing gift and thank God for Jesus' sacrifice on the cross?

Worship

Opening Song(s): Open your time together with 3–5 songs of praise and worship that support the theme of celebration and sacrifice. Possibilities include "How Great Thou Art," "All Hail the Power of Jesus' Name," "Joy to the World," "How Great Is Our God," and "Be Glorified."

Scripture Reading: Ecclesiastes 3:1-8

Time of Prayer: Ask participants to share joys and concerns, or use Psalm 145 as a call and response reading and close with prayer.

Closing Song: "Wondrous Love" ("What wondrous love is this") or "Amazing Love/You Are My King"

Fellowship

After worship, gather people together at the long worktables outside your kitchen. Participants can now decorate the king cakes. If coloring the frosting, the station host can make batches of green, purple, and gold frosting ahead of time by adding food coloring to tubs of white frosting. The easier method is to let families frost the cake with white frosting and then sprinkle on green-, purple-, and gold-colored sugar in three sections. If serving a full meal first, set out the frosted king cakes for dessert.

Note: Remind participants to watch out for the baby/raisin hidden in the cake!

March | Women's History Month

In 1987 the United States Congress set apart March as a month for education and celebration around women's accomplishments in history. For more ideas and background information, visit www.smithsonianeducation.org/educators/resource_library/women_resources.html.

• **Christian Women in History.** Choose four historically significant Christian women and create weekly intergenerational programming, exploring a different woman and her contributions to history each week (see sample program at www.forallgenerations.com).

• **Telling HerStory.** Design an intergenerational program featuring a living history storyteller or a dramatic volunteer who will present a monologue or brief skit about a famous woman in your community, your congregation, or in Scripture. (For biblical women, consider using *Meet Bathsheba* or *Meet the Queen of Sheba,* both by Roseanne Gartner, published by Judson Press.)

After the presentation, facilitate a small-group discussion about the woman's life. Be sure to have a table with more information about the woman (e.g., map showing her birthplace, samples of any books, poetry, or songs she may have written, an image of her and other items that signify her achievements. And particularly for the hands-on learners in your group (including children), offer a station where participants can do a related art or craft activity.

CHAPTER 5

March
Ash Wednesday

Program Focus: The temptation of Jesus

Key Verse: "'Worship the Lord your God, and serve only him'" (Matthew 4:10 NRSV).

Purpose:
a. To introduce/reintroduce participants to the historical Christian roots of Ash Wednesday/Lent
b. To explore the story of Jesus' 40 days of temptation in the wilderness
c. To encourage participants to use the 40 days of Lent as a time for spiritual self-reflection and confession of sin and as a time to refocus on what they need to do to grow as Christians

Leader Background

In *Creative Programs for the Church Year*, Malcolm Shotwell explains the season of Lent:

> Lent is an Anglo-Saxon word, meaning "spring." Originally the Lenten season referred to the springtime awakening observed in all cultures. Down through the centuries, various Christian church leaders have seen the need for a time in the church year when Christians would think deeply on the meaning of Easter as symbolized by the cross, the empty tomb, and changed lives. Thus, the Lenten season referring to the coming of spring was encompassed with a religious significance. Not only would people now think of this season of the year as preparation for the coming of spring on earth, but also the coming of new spiritual life.
>
> The period of Lent is forty days on the Christian calendar, that is, forty days before Easter, excluding Sundays. These forty days parallel the forty days Jesus spent in the wilderness following his baptism, the forty days in which Jesus thought through the purpose for life, his mission, and his God-ordained goals. If Jesus had need for devotional discipline, how much more do we? (Judson Press, 1986, 28)

As a side note, Lent does not officially count Sundays during the 40-day period, because each Sunday is already considered a celebration of our risen Lord. Christians who receive the sign of the cross on their foreheads with ashes on Ash Wednesday do so because the cross and the ashes remind us that someday our human bodies will return to ashes, but our souls will live with Jesus forever if we accept him as our Lord and Savior.

Worship

Opening Song(s): Open your time together with 3–5 songs of praise and worship that support the theme of drawing closer to God. Possibilities include "When I Survey the Wondrous Cross," "Great Is Thy Faithfulness," "Blest Be the Tie That Binds," "Lord, I Lift Your Name on High," "The Heart of Worship," "Here I Am to Worship," "Jesus, Draw Me Close."

Scripture Reading: Use the acronym LENT to guide participants through the Scripture reading. The leader will read the statement, and the congregation will read the corresponding passages. The leader will also introduce the actions to the group and invite them to do the same motions.

Leader: People of God, join me in learning about Lent. Lent is a time to LAY down your burdens and admit your sin. Lay those burdens down. (Leader pantomimes holding a big rock, struggling with it, and setting it down on the ground.)

People: And Jesus said . . . (People read Matthew 11:28-30.)

Leader: Lent is a time to EXIT the wilderness of sin and temptation. Leave bad choices behind. (Leader pantomimes marching.)

People: (People read Deuteronomy 6:4-9.)

Leader: Lent is a time to NURTURE your spirit. Take care of the body and soul God gave you. (Leader pantomimes hugging self and patting self on arm.)

People: May we live according to Paul's prayer for us: (People read Ephesians 3:16-19.)

Leader: Lent is a time to TRANSFORM your life. Be open to God's will for your life. (Leader starts with arms crossed over chest and then opens them up and out over his or her head, stretching hands to heaven.)

People: (People read Romans 12:2.)

Time of Prayer: Pray with a special focus on taking time to listen to God and letting God be at work in God's people.

Closing Song: "Day by Day" or "Be Thou My Vision"

Faith Stations

Station 1. Temptation in the Wilderness

What You'll Need

Volunteer: station host

Bibles

Index cards

Pens/pencils

Storytelling supplies

Large, low rectangular tub filled with 2–3" of sand to represent the desert wilderness

Pile of small pebbles to represent the stones

White box approximately 6" x 6" x 6" to represent the temple

Stack of bricks or building blocks covered with a green and/or brown cloth to represent the mountain

Small action figure dressed in a tunic to represent Jesus

Small action figure dressed in a white tunic to represent the angel

Small action figure dressed in a black or red tunic to represent the devil

The station host should welcome participants and invite them to gather around the storytelling sandbox. Have smaller children sit up front on the floor in a semicircle around the box. Older children and adults can make a ring of chairs behind the little ones.

Introduce the story of the temptation of Jesus in the wilderness and explain that the 40 days in Lent symbolize the 40 days that Jesus spent in the wilderness praying and preparing to serve God. For Christians Ash Wednesday marks the beginning of Lent, which is a time of praying and preparing our hearts to draw closer to God and to serve God. Lent is a time to acknowledge the choices we make in our life that are not God-honoring and work on getting right with God by seeking forgiveness and trying to live according to Jesus' example.

Then tell (not read) the story of Jesus in the wilderness using the props listed above.

After the story, pass out Bibles and ask the group the following questions:

1. Even though Jesus had been fasting (not eating) for 40 days, he refused to use God's power to turn the stones into bread. How did Jesus respond to the devil (see Matthew 4:3)?

2. When the devil dared Jesus to jump from the temple roof, what did Jesus say to him (see Matthew 4:7)?

3. When the devil offered to give Jesus power over all earthly kingdoms if he would worship the devil, how did Jesus respond (see Matthew 4:10)?

4. What kind of weapon did Jesus use to fight temptation?

5. What Scriptures might you use as weapons to fight temptation?

Station 2. True Confessions

What You'll Need

Volunteer: station host

Index cards

Pens/pencils

Aluminum baking sheets

Hot pads/towels

Cooling racks

Taper candles with holders

Matches

Aluminum foil squares (1 per family group)

Larry Boy and the Bad Apple DVD (Big Idea Productions, 2006)

TV/DVD player

This station should be set up with long worktables. Each table should have set up for every family group a baking tray on a hot pad/towel/cooling rack (to protect the table) and lined with a fresh square of foil. Candles and matches should be available on each table, too, along with a supply of index cards and pens and pencils. The station host should welcome the group and ask them to sit at the tables in their family groups. If you have singles or older adults who have joined with a family, keep those groups together but give an index card to each person. Position the TV/DVD player so that participants can all view it from their seats.

Preface the video with an explanation that from the time of Adam and Eve, we humans have lived with broken relationships. Often we break our relationship with God, even temporarily, because of our sin or the things we do that are not pleasing to God. This sin pushes us away from God. To reconnect and restore our friendship with God, we need to seek God's forgiveness. Today, at the start of Lent, we have the perfect opportunity to talk to God about our sin and seek his forgiveness.

Show the first half of the VeggieTales movie *Larry Boy and the Bad Apple*. Then ask family groups to discuss the following questions:

1. Who or what was tempting Larry Boy and his friends in Bumblyburg?

2. What kind of problems was the Bad Apple causing for the friends?

3. Think about times when you were tempted to disobey God's Word and God's will. What happened? Talk about these choices with your family group and discuss what happened.

4. Because we are human and are not perfect like Jesus, we make mistakes over and over again. We give in to temptation. We fail to follow God's Word. We forget to be more like Jesus. Think about a time when you gave in to temptation and did not make a God-honoring choice. Did you ever ask for forgiveness from the person you hurt? From God? Now is the time to get right with God. Take an index card and write down one thing for which you need to ask God's forgiveness. (Parents can help children.) These do not need to be shared. These thoughts are between you and God. Fold the index card in half when finished.

5. *Note:* This step requires adult supervision. An adult in the group can light a candle. One person at a time can set their index card on the foil square and touch the candle to it so that it begins to burn. As soon as it has burned, the next person can place his or her card on the foil and repeat the process. When all cards in your group are burned, blow out the candle and use the tip to spread the ashes out so they cool. While they are cooling, have someone in your group say a prayer asking God to forgive the participants for the sins they've shared with him and make their hearts new and clean.

When the ashes are cool, you can use them to make the sign of a cross on the back of your hand to remind you that you are working on your friendship with God. If you want to save some ashes to take home, wrap them up in the foil. Share with the group the information from the Leader Background section at the beginning of the chapter, especially in terms of the significance of the ashes.

Station 3. Finding Your True North

What You'll Need

Volunteer: station host

Bibles

Mini compasses (four to five total, need to be magnetized and functional, can be bought for $3–$4 each at a sporting goods store; or ask ahead of time if congregation members have compasses you can borrow for this activity)

Assorted maps (need to be able to lay flat)

Assorted refrigerator magnets

Business card–size magnet for craft activity (one per family group)

Card stock cut to the magnet size

Sticky back foam circles and crosses (optional)

Permanent markers

Ahead of time, the host should set up this station with one map taped to the wall. Set one compass and an assortment of magnets nearby. Set up the other mini-stations around the room either on the floor or on tables. Each station needs a map, a compass, and an assortment of magnets.

Welcome the group and gather the participants around the map on the wall. Explain that in this station participants are going to be exploring the concept of true north, which is the direction a functional compass will always point.

Ask for a handful of volunteers. The first person will hold the compass on the map. The other volunteers should indicate which way the compass arrow is pointing. That is true north. Then hand those volunteers each a magnet and ask them to move the magnets around the compass. As they do, the magnets will affect the compass magnet, which will no longer be able to indicate true north.

Ask, "If you were out in the wilderness and your compass wasn't able to tell you true north anymore, what would happen?"

Send family groups out to the map stations and ask them to experiment with finding true north and then alter true north by moving the magnets around the compass. After a few minutes, ask the groups to discuss this question: "Magnets affect a compass's ability to show true north. If God is our true north, what things in our life are like the magnets? What throws us off course? What distracts us from letting God be our guide in life?"

Once groups have had a few minutes to discuss, invite them to make a true north magnet. Using business card–size sticky-face magnets, family groups can place a business card–size piece of card stock on the front of the magnet. Then they can either draw a compass or use a sticky-back craft foam circle to form the compass, adding the directions and an arrow with a permanent marker. They can also add a cross and/or the sayings: "God is my true north!" and/or "Lead us not into temptation, but deliver us from the evil one" (Matthew 6:13 NIV).

Fellowship

Ideally this program should close with a time of fellowship; however, your planning team will need to decide how you want your event to flow. Do you want to start with a meal, then go to the faith stations, and close with worship? Or do you want to open with worship, go to the faith stations, and end with punch and cookies? Each event can be tailored to your group's needs and time constraints. Just be sure to include a time of fellowship in your program, whether a full meal or light refreshments.

Note: If you are closing your time with fellowship, you can also show the second half of *Larry Boy and the Bad Apple* in your gathering area.

CHAPTER 6

March
St. Patrick's Day

Program Focus: St. Patrick the missionary

Key Verse: "'Go therefore and make disciples of all nations, baptizing them in the name of the Father and of the Son and of the Holy Spirit'" (Matthew 28:19 NRSV).

Purpose:
a. To explore the historical Christian roots of St. Patrick (who he was and what he did to serve God)
b. To identify examples of other missionaries (past and present)
c. To make a personal "next step" for going out to make disciples

Leader Background

Come March 17 many Americans turn a little green, celebrating St. Patrick's Day regardless of their religious or ethnic heritage. Yet it's more than likely that few people really know the true story of St. Patrick and the value of his contributions to the Christian faith. While people may be aware of the term *saint* as it is used by Roman Catholics, they may not understand how it fits into their faith traditions. In Catholicism, saints are honored people, Christians who have lived faithful lives above and beyond the call of duty. After their deaths, these Christians go through a canonization process, whereby the Roman Catholic Church determines whether they are worthy of sainthood by virtue of their extremely honorable and faithful lives and/or their martyrdom because of their faithful living. In addition, the candidate for sainthood must have performed at least two verified miracles. The pope is the one who grants sainthood. This formal process started around AD 900.

The Bible refers to saints both in the Old and New Testaments. In the Old Testament, the saints are God's holy and chosen people who put their faith in him. "You are to be holy to me because I, the LORD, am holy, and have set you apart from the nations to be my own" we read in Leviticus 20:26 (NIV). And in Psalm 31:23-24 we hear, "Love the LORD, all his saints! The LORD preserves the faithful, but the proud he pays back in full. Be strong and take heart, all you who hope in the LORD" (NIV).

In the New Testament, saints are all those who follow Jesus. Paul opens the first letter to the Corinthians by saying, "To the church of God that is in Corinth, to those who are sanctified in Christ Jesus, called to be saints, together with all those who in every place call on the name of our Lord Jesus Christ, both their Lord and ours" (1 Corinthians 1:2 NRSV). And in Ephesians 1:17-19, Paul says, "I keep asking that the God of our Lord Jesus Christ, the glorious Father, may give you the Spirit of wisdom and revelation, so that you may know him better. I pray also that the eyes of your heart may be enlightened in order that you may know the hope to which he has called you, the riches of his glorious inheritance in the saints, and his incomparably great power for us who believe" (NIV). Saints are all of God's children, the faithful who have gone before and those who follow Jesus now.

Patrick was made a saint because of his faithful discipleship. He understood Jesus' call to go out and make disciples of all nations. Like Jesus, that became his life's work. In this program, participants will get to know Patrick better and see him as a model for faithful living, not just the once-a-year hero in a secular celebration.

Note: Fellowship will also include part of the faith education for this program. Ahead of time, the planning team needs to contact a variety of missionaries who can come and share their stories. These can be people working in the local mission field in your area, people working in urban mission settings in a nearby city, or people from your denomination who have worked in foreign mission fields. Invite these missionaries to come and go through the station rotations with your participants and then enjoy a meal with them during fellowship time (see additional notes at end).

Worship

Opening Song(s): Open your time together with 3–5 songs of praise and worship that support the theme of discipleship and disciple-making. Possibilities include "Be Thou My Vision," "Amazing Grace," "I'm Gonna Live So God Can Use Me," "Take My Life," "Shout to the Lord."

Scripture Reading: Matthew 28:16-21

Time of Prayer: Ask participants to share joys and concerns and/or the leader can pray with a special emphasis on mission work and missionaries. The leader can also invite the guest speaker missionaries to come forward, and participants can gather around them and lay hands on them during the prayer time.

Closing Song: "Children, Go Where I Send Thee" or "Here I Am, Lord"

Faith Stations

Station 1. St. Patrick and St. Paul

Note: If your total group is larger than 35–40 participants, consider having one St. Patrick/St. Paul station for each group of 35. Groups need to do Station 1 first, followed by Station 2, followed by the fellowship time with the guest missionaries. Active learning will more easily take place if the storytelling can be done in groups of fewer than 35.

What You'll Need

Volunteer: station host
Robe costume for St. Patrick
Tunic costume for St. Paul
Irish flag (color photocopy is fine)
6' section of rope
Shepherd's crook and toy sheep
Rubber snake
Cross
Calendar with the year AD 450 written across it
Pitcher of water
Yellow legal pad
Bible
Shamrock (a paper cutout is fine, or cut a stem off of a shamrock plant)

The station host should be dressed as (New Testament) Paul and should welcome participants to the storytelling session, asking them to gather in a semicircle. Ask the group some brainstorming questions about St. Patrick's Day: Who was St. Patrick? Why do people celebrate this holiday? In what ways do they celebrate?

Then explain that today people are going to learn the true story of St. Patrick and why he deserves to be honored as a faithful servant of God. Participants will hear two stories. The first will be from St. Patrick himself. Select a volunteer who is willing to participate in an interactive trivia contest and also be a reader. The volunteer can put on the costume robe.

Take the volunteer aside and explain that they are going to play a St. Patrick's trivia game, and the host will be handing the volunteer props to hold. The volunteer should play along.

Explain that participants are going to do a trivia contest about St. Patrick. Divide the group into two teams. They can huddle to decide on their group answer. All statements are true or false. Ask each team their answer and keep score.

1. St. Patrick was born in Ireland. (Host hands volunteer the Irish flag to hold. *False; he was born in England.*)

2. St. Patrick was kidnapped and sold into slavery. (Host ties rope around volunteer and leads him a few steps away. *True; as a teenager.*)

3. St. Patrick worked as a shepherd. (Host hands volunteer a crook and sheep. *True; this was while in slavery.*)

4. St. Patrick chased the snakes out of Ireland. (Host hands volunteer a rubber snake. *False; that's just a legend.*)

5. St. Patrick had a born-again/conversion experience. (Host hands volunteer a cross. *True; after returning to England from captivity.*)

6. St. Patrick was a missionary in the fifth century. (Host hands volunteer a calendar with AD 450 written on it. *True; probably in the mid-400s.*)

7. St. Patrick baptized everyone in the River Shannon. (Host pours a few sprinkles of water on volunteer's head. *False; that's just a legend.*)

8. St. Patrick studied to be a lawyer. (Host hands volunteer a legal pad. *False; he studied to be a priest.*)

9. St. Patrick was a missionary in Ireland for about 30 years. (Host hands volunteer a Bible. *True.*)

10. St. Patrick gave everyone he met a shamrock. (Host hands volunteer a shamrock. *False; legend says he used the shamrock to teach about the Trinity.*)

After the trivia contest, the volunteer should then read the following excerpt taken from St. Patrick's Confession in his or her best dramatic interpretation and Irish brogue. (Text is in the public domain and can be accessed through http://www.ccel.org/ccel/patrick/confession.all.html.)

I am Patrick, a sinner, most unlearned, the least of all the faithful, and utterly despised by many. I was taken into captivity to Ireland with many thousands of people—and deservedly so, because we turned away from God and did not keep His commandments. . . . And there the Lord opened the sense of my unbelief that I might at last remember my sins and be converted with all my heart to the Lord my God. . . . Hence I cannot be silent—nor, indeed is it expedient—about the great benefits and the great grace which the Lord has deigned to bestow upon me in the land of my captivity; for this we can give to God in return after having been chastened by Him, to exalt and praise His wonders before every nation that is anywhere under the heaven.

Thus I give untiring thanks to God who kept me faithful in the day of my temptation, so that today I may confidently offer my soul as a living sacrifice for Christ my Lord; who am I, Lord? or, rather, what is my calling? that you appeared to me in so great a divine quality . . . so that I might imitate one of those whom, once, long ago, the Lord already preordained to be heralds of his gospel to witness to all peoples to the ends of the earth. So are we seeing, and so it is fulfilled; behold, we are witnesses because the Gospel has been preached as far as the places beyond which no man lives.

After St. Patrick's story, step up and tell Paul's conversion story from Acts 9:1-20. Preface the story with the fact that Paul, who was a faithful missionary for years and who wrote much of the New Testament, had actually, like St. Patrick, fallen away from God. Before accepting Jesus, Paul spent part of his life hunting down Christians and putting them in prison. However, one day on the road to Damascus, Saul (as he was called then) had an amazing experience that changed his heart (tell story).

After the story, ask participants if anyone has questions, and address them before directing them to move to Station 2.

Station 2. Saintly Shamrocks

What You'll Need

Volunteer: station host

1 Saintly Shamrock handout per family group
   (see www.forallgenerations.com for PDF sample)

Pens

Flip chart/whiteboard and markers

This station should be set up with long worktables. Each table should be set with handouts and pens. The host should welcome the group and ask them to sit at the tables in their family groups. If you have singles or older adults who have joined with a family, keep those groups together, but be sure to provide a handout for each head of household.

Use the flip chart or whiteboard to write down group answers to this question: "How would you define the word *saint*?"

Introduce the main activity by first sharing the saint information from the Leader Background section. Then ask: "How do Paul's and Patrick's lives seem similar? How do Paul and Patrick fit the description of saint according to what we've learned and what we've listed? Are there any other people in the Bible you think share these same qualities?" (Write down additional names on the flip chart.)

Then ask the family groups each to take a Saintly Shamrock handout and give these directions:

1. Using the descriptions we've come up with for the word *saint*, think of a Bible character you admire and write his or her name in one leaf of your shamrock, along with the saintly quality you admire. Table groups should share their answers.

2. Next, think of one real-life person who shows saintly qualities. Write his or her name in the second leaf, along with the saintly quality you admire. It's okay to write more than one name and one quality. Again, share your answers.

3. Last, write down each person's name in the third leaf. Talk about what saintly quality each person would like to have and write it next to that person's name. If you have time, explain to your group why you'd like to have that quality.

Station 3. A Missionary Meal

What You'll Need

Volunteers: station host, missionary guest speakers
   (1 per every 8–10 participants), volunteers to serve
   the meal

Dinner (salad and rolls, main meal, dessert)

The station host should welcome participants to the meal and invite them to be seated at the dinner tables. Formally introduce the missionary guest speakers to the group and invite a missionary to sit at each dinner table. Dinner will consist of three courses: salad and rolls, main entrée, and dessert. During each course (which will be served by volunteers), the missionary at the table will have 15–20 minutes to talk at the table about his or her experiences. After 15–20 minutes, ring a bell, and the missionaries will get up and switch tables while the volunteers bring out the next course. Repeat through dessert. After dessert, the fellowship time can continue with people getting up and moving around the room to talk more with the missionaries.

Missionaries can also be invited to set up display tables ahead of time with pictures and information about their mission sites. They can staff these tables after dinner and continue speaking with participants. The planning team may also want to consider taking up a free-will offering in conjunction with this program that can be divided among the missionaries who are joining you.

Note: For grace, you might want to use the "Prayer for the Faithful" by Saint Patrick: Search online for "Prayer for the Faithful" and "St. Patrick" or see the link on this book's website (www.forall generations.com).

Fellowship

Note: The missionary dinner serves as your fellowship portion of the program.

Extension Activity

To follow up on this program, your planning team might want to offer an off-site field trip to one of your local missionary's work sites or sponsor an off-site missions workday.

CHAPTER 7

April
Maundy Thursday

Program Focus: Understanding Communion

Key Verses: "Then he took a loaf of bread, and when he had given thanks, he broke it and gave it to them, saying, 'This is my body, which is given for you. Do this in remembrance of me.' And he did the same with the cup after supper, saying, 'This cup that is poured out for you is the new covenant in my blood'" (Luke 22:19-20 NRSV).

Purpose:
a. To introduce/reintroduce the story of the Last Supper
b. To explore the concept of Jesus' death bringing life
c. To explore the concept of how communion strengthens our connection to Jesus through our forgiveness of sins

Leader Background

Maundy Thursday takes place during Holy Week and marks the Last Supper that Jesus shared with his disciples. Jesus' words shared during this meal became the basis for the Christian sacrament of communion. Of course, Jesus' disciples didn't know they were experiencing communion; they were there, as faithful Jews, to share in the Passover supper with Jesus.

Passover, in the Jewish tradition, is the celebration of God rescuing his people from Egyptian slavery. Passover literally marked the night that God's angel of death passed over the Jewish homes but struck down all firstborn Egyptian sons. God then sent his people into the wilderness, following their leader Moses, to seek freedom in the land of milk and honey that God had promised them.

Worship

Opening Song(s): Open your time together with 3–5 songs of praise and worship that support the theme of being connected to Jesus. Possibilities include "All Hail the Power of Jesus' Name," "Let Us Break Bread Together," "When I Survey the Wondrous Cross," "Nothing but the Blood," "Mighty to Save," "Jesus Messiah."

Scripture Reading: Exodus 12:21-28

Time of Prayer: Ask participants to share joys and concerns and/or the leader can pray with a special emphasis on our friendship with Jesus Christ.

Closing Song: "You Are My All in All" or "What a Friend We Have in Jesus"

Faith Stations

Station 1. Exploring the Seder Supper

What You'll Need

Volunteer: station host

Elements of the seder (prepare 1 tray per 6–10 people: hard-boiled egg, a lamb bone or other symbolic bone, matzoh, parsley, horseradish spread, charoset, small dish of saltwater, grape juice in individual cups)

Tablecloths and napkins

White candle and matches for each tray

2 packets yeast

1 slice of yeast bread

Hand-washing supplies (pitcher of water, large bowl, and towel for each group of 6–10 people)

Ahead of time, this station should be set up with tables prepared with tablecloths and napkins. One seder tray and 1 hand-washing set should be laid out for each group of 6–10 people. The station host should welcome guests to the station and invite them to sit at the tables.

Introduce the experience by reminding participants that Jesus and his Jewish friends would have celebrated the Passover supper each year, just as God commanded in the Exodus reading they heard during worship. Seder is the name for the meal and the accompanying prayers, songs, and readings from Scripture. *Seder* means "order," and the celebration does have a set order. However, during this program, guests will be experiencing only a few select pieces of the seder. It will give them only a taste of the seder experience and is not designed to replace a full seder experience.

Note: for more background knowledge or to learn how to offer a full Christian seder dinner, go to www.cresourcei.org/haggadah.html or www.christianseder.com.

Walk participants through the symbolic seder. Ahead of time, the host will have hidden the yeast packet in the room. Hold up a duplicate packet so children know what to search for and explain that yeast is what makes leavened bread rise so it doesn't look like matzoh (hold up samples of leavened and unleavened bread). Explain that one of God's rules about the Passover feast was that no leavening, such as yeast, could be in the home. This reminded God's people that they had to make and eat unleavened bread—or matzoh—for seven days when God rescued them from slavery in Egypt. Invite the children to find the packet.

After the yeast has been found, ask the adults (traditionally the mother) at the tables to light the candles to begin the seder. An adult can also pour a small cup of grape juice for each person to drink after the host says a short prayer. Pray that God will help people faithfully remember his promises of freedom, deliverance, redemption, and thanksgiving that he made to our Bible ancestors and that he still makes to us.

Next, ask participants to use the hand-washing supplies to wash the hands of the person seated next to them. One person will place his or her hands over the bowl while the other pours a little water over them and then dries them with the towel. Everyone should have a turn washing and being washed. While people are doing this, read from John 13:1-17.

After the hand washing, explain the different elements on the seder tray. Participants are welcome to taste the elements as the host explains them.

1. *The parsley and the saltwater.* The parsley symbolizes life. God creates all life, and we take joy in that. The saltwater symbolizes the tears that come when life gets difficult and challenging. Dip the parsley in the saltwater and taste.

2. *The matzoh.* This is the unleavened bread that our Bible ancestors prepared before their journey to freedom. We eat this bread to remember their bondage and God's rescuing them from slavery. We eat this bread to remember that Jesus frees us from our sins. Taste the matzoh.

3. *The lamb bone and egg.* The lamb bone reminds us of the lamb that was sacrificed and of its blood marking the doorposts of the Israelites' homes so that God's angel of death would pass over them. The egg reminds us of the sacrifices that used to be made at the temple in Jerusalem. The egg is also a symbol of new life. Because Jesus died for our sins, we receive the gift of eternal life through our faith in him. Taste the egg.

4. *The horseradish.* This bitter herb reminds us of the difficult times the Israelites endured in slavery, as well as the difficult times in our own lives. Taste the horseradish.

5. *The charoset.* This sweet mix reminds us of the joy that God brings to our lives, even when we are in the middle of sadness and struggle. Taste the charoset. See www.forallgenerations.com for recipe.

When the host is through explaining the seder tray, an adult should blow out the candle. Participants can resample any of the tray items if there are leftovers. Used trays should be cleared and tables reset for the next group.

Station 2. Songs and Games

What You'll Need

Volunteer: station host
Song sheets and game props as needed

This station should be set up with a circle of chairs. After inviting participants to have a seat, the host will explain that a seder (Passover) meal includes singing and playing games. Ahead of time, prepare a list of fun and easy songs that are familiar to the congregation. Have song sheets or songbooks ready, and if possible have a musician and song leader on hand to help with this part of the program.

After singing several songs, the host should invite the group to play a few games. Upset the Fruit Basket will work well with your circle. In this game, the host assigns a fruit name to each person (use three different names). One person is "It" and stands in the middle of the circle. Remove "Its"'s chair before starting play. "It" calls one fruit. All people assigned to that fruit stand up and switch chairs. "It" tries to find a new seat. Whoever is left without a seat becomes the new "It." "It" can also call "Upset the fruit basket," which means that everyone has to get up and find a new seat at the same time.

Another good game, if you have the space, is Hide-and-Seek, as it picks up the theme of hiding and seeking the leaven before the start of the seder. If you don't have room for Hide-and-Seek, play Hot and Cold. One player ("It") leaves the room. The host hides the "treasure." When "It" returns, he or she may ask each remaining player for one clue as to the location of the treasure. The other players may only respond, "Hot" or "Cold." For example, "It" might ask, "Is the treasure by the window?" and the responder would answer "Hot" if the treasure was near the window or "Cold" if the treasure was nowhere near the window.

End this station rotation with a few more songs.

Station 3. Communion Connection

What You'll Need

Volunteer: station host
Tunic/robe costume
3 loaves of bread (1 for each rotation)
Clear glass filled with grape juice
Large sheet of mural paper (4' wide by 8' high)
   with a large cross (cross beams should be 2' wide)
   drawn on it
Pink construction paper hearts about 6" wide
Markers
Tape
Grapes and pretzels to share
Praise and worship music CD
CD player

The station host (dressed in the tunic/robe) will welcome participants and invite them to gather in a semicircle. Explain that you will be telling the story of the Last Supper from Peter's point of view. Peter was one of the twelve disciples who was with Jesus in the upper room for the Last Supper in Jerusalem. Jesus' own words and actions during the Last Supper now symbolize the Christian sacrament of communion.

Note: The host will not be serving communion during this station but will help people explore why this sacrament is central to the Christian faith.

Tell the Last Supper story as Peter, using the Luke 22:7-30 and John 13:34-35 texts as a base and using the props of the loaf of bread and the glass of grape juice (wine). When finished, ask the group to form small groups to answer the following questions:

1. What does Jesus mean when he tells us to love one another as he has loved us?

2. How have you shown Jesus-love to another person?

3. If Jesus-love means that we get do-overs and second chances when we make mistakes (we get a new life free from sin), what does that mean for our relationships with friends and family members when we make mistakes with them?

After groups have had 5–10 minutes to answer this question, invite them to add their answers to the mural by writing words or drawing pictures on the paper hearts (they might include words like *kindness, forgiveness, compassion, understanding, patience,* and *service* or pictures of helping one another, caring for one another, visiting an elderly person, being kind to an enemy, etc.). Have praise and worship music playing in the background while people work. After they tape their hearts to the mural, they can enjoy the grapes and pretzels and socialize with one another, much as Jesus would have done before and during the final meal he shared with his friends.

Fellowship

Ideally, this program includes a full meal (after the station rotations) to symbolize the time that Jesus spent eating and sharing faith traditions with his disciples; however, your planning team will need to decide how you want your event to flow. Do you want to start with a meal, then go to the faith stations, and close with worship? Or do you want to open with worship, go to the faith stations, and end with punch and cookies? Each event can be tailored to your group's needs and time constraints. Just be sure to include a time of fellowship in your program, whether a full meal or light refreshments.

CHAPTER 8

April
Volunteer Celebration

Leader Background

Although Jesus was the Son of God, he repeatedly told his followers, "The Son of Man came not to be served but to serve" (Matthew 20:28 NRSV). Church ministries cannot function without the volunteers who model Christlike servanthood as they offer their gifts and talents to the church and the larger community. While these individuals are not serving to get the recognition, it is important to lift up their contributions, thank them for their service, and use them as models of faithful discipleship.

Note: Ahead of time, the planning team should make a list of all of the church volunteers, as well as public servants in your community whom your church would like to recognize. The planning team should send out invitations to these individuals, inviting them to a short worship service and reception on the date of your program. Your fellowship time today will actually be the volunteer recognition reception. Make the food as simple or as elaborate as your budget and kitchen crew will allow.

Program Focus: Volunteers model servanthood

Key Verse: "'The Son of Man came not to be served but to serve'" (Mark 10:45 NRSV).

Purpose:
a. To explore examples of servanthood in the Bible: Jesus, Daniel, Rahab, Boaz
b. To thank all volunteers who serve in God's name
c. To create a personal "next step" to volunteer for God

Faith Stations

Station 1. Super Servants

What You'll Need

Volunteer: station host

Bible-time costumes for kids and adults (including robes/tunics, crowns, lion masks, and a red cord)

Bibles with list of drama passages (Jesus and Zacchaeus, Luke 19:1-10; The Good Samaritan, Luke 10:25-37; Rahab Saves the Spies, Joshua 2:1-24; Daniel in the Lions' Den, Daniel 6:1-25; Boaz Cares for Ruth, Ruth 2:1-16)

The host should welcome participants and explain that they will be acting out stories of faithful servants of God in the Bible. Family groups can split up or combine if needed. The easiest way to act out these stories is to have a reader-narrator read the passage and have actors pantomime the actions and/or say their characters' lines. Try to give all group members a part even if they are just members of the crowd or other travelers along the road.

The host should ask families to find a work space, read their stories out loud, assign parts, and begin practice. The host should be familiar with the stories and circulate while groups are working. The Zacchaeus story illustrates that Jesus wasn't afraid to help those who were looked down on by most people. His mission was to serve all of God's children, even the most unlovable. In the story of the Good Samaritan, the culturally unpopular Samaritan showed mercy and kindness to the injured traveler when other well-respected citizens passed by the man without stopping to help. The Daniel story illustrates that staying faithful to God is what a true servant of God does, even in difficult times. The Rahab story shows how God uses the most unlikely people to serve him and be examples of true discipleship. The Ruth and Boaz story illustrates true kindness and compassion for others, along with the values of responsibility and commitment.

The host should give groups 15–20 minutes to work. Groups can then present their skits. Each rotation should choose one skit to represent their large group during worship at the end of the program. Make sure all three of the skits are different stories.

Station 2. Appreciation Preparation

What You'll Need

Volunteer: station host

Food and decorations for the volunteer reception (see below)

Thank-you card supplies (fancy paper or blank note cards, markers, stickers, glue sticks, glitter, Bibles and concordances or a preselected list of encouraging "appreciation" Scriptures, list of invited volunteers, etc.)

This station will vary depending on how extravagant the planning team has decided to make the volunteer appreciation reception. However, each group that rotates through the station can be involved in decorating the gathering area with balloons and streamers. Family groups can make thank-you cards for each invited volunteer. Groups can also assist in decorating cookies and cupcakes, cutting up fresh fruits and vegetables for snacks, or even preparing a full dinner if desired. The station host should work with the kitchen crew to make sure each rotation shares in the work.

Station 3. Volunteer Venue

What You'll Need

Volunteer: station host

Table and chair for each invited ministry and community organization (including any Christian camps in your area)

Table coverings for each table

Blank construction paper

Pens/markers

Sheets of preprinted return address labels that have each organization or ministry name, contact person, and phone number and website listed (each ministry or organization will get one or more sheets of these labels, depending on your total group size).

Note: Ahead of time, the planning team should invite all the church's ministries to come and staff a table at the Volunteer Appreciation program. They may also choose to invite local community organizations who use volunteers. All of these representatives should also be invited to the reception following the station rotations. In addition, assuming your attendees will be a mixed group of families with children, singles, older adults, teens, etc., make sure that your volunteer opportunities will cover this range of ages and abilities.

The station host should welcome participants to the Volunteer Venue (if possible, set up in the same room where you will hold your appreciation reception) and explain that they will have the chance to meet and greet the leaders of the various ministries at your church and organizations in your community that use volunteers. Before they start, ask each person to trace and cut out their own hand. Participants will take these hands around to the various tables. If they find an opportunity they'd like to be involved in, they can ask for a contact information sticker to be placed on their hand cutouts.

Note: Ministries and organizations will also likely want to have a sign-up sheet on their tables, as well as other information and pictures describing how they use volunteers.

Worship

Opening Song(s): Open your time together with 3–5 songs of praise and worship that support the theme of serving Jesus and serving others. Possibilities include "Here I Am, Lord," "'Tis the Gift to Be Simple," "Joyful, Joyful, We Adore Thee," "Give Us Clean Hands," "From the Inside Out."

Scripture Reading: John 13:12-20

Time of Prayer: Ask participants to share joys and concerns. Pray for those concerns as well as giving thanks for all who use their gifts to serve God.

Dramas: To add to your appreciation service, each rotation group can perform the drama they selected to share during worship. The worship leader can explain that these are all stories that show God's faithful servants in action.

Closing Song: "O Master, Let Me Walk with Thee" or "Everyday"

Fellowship

Ideally this program will close with a time of fellowship after worship in the gathering area participants have prepared and with the snacks they have created to thank all the volunteers who are being recognized for their service (see Station 2). However, your planning team will need to decide how you want your event to flow. Just be sure to include a time of fellowship in your event.

April | National Humor Month / April Fool's Day

Celebrate National Humor Month with a Feast of Fools! Host an intergenerational talent show and combine it with a potluck meal before or after the show. Invite congregation members of all ages to perform musical numbers, dance routines, poetry readings, standup comedy, dramatic skits, and more. Emphasize the comedic element of the night, and consider making placards with joy- or laughter-related Scriptures part of your table centerpieces.

CHAPTER 9

April
Earth Day

Program Focus: Caring for God's Creation

Key Verse: "God blessed them, and God said to them, 'Be fruitful and multiply, and fill the earth and subdue it'" (Genesis 1:28 NRSV).

Purpose:
a. To introduce/reintroduce God's plan for humankind to care for the earth
b. To explore what it means to be a steward of creation
c. To make a personal "next step" to care for creation

Leader Background

Earth Day has been a national holiday in the United States since April 22, 1970, thanks to Senator Gaylord Nelson, who saw a need to increase public awareness in how we treat the earth. Since that time, numerous organizations have been founded to offer programming and resources in conjunction with Earth Day. In particular, faith-based initiatives related to eco-justice have been growing. Visit http://www.eco-justice.org/denom.asp for a list of mainline denominations' eco-justice websites, or visit The National Religious Partnership for the Environment at http://www.nrpe.org/index.html for many more resources and program ideas.

Worship

Opening Song(s): Open your time together with 3–5 songs of praise and worship that support the theme of God's creation. Possibilities include "All Creatures of Our God and King," "For the Beauty of the Earth," "O Beautiful for Spacious Skies," "God of Wonders," "Awesome God," "Creation."

Scripture Reading: Psalm 100 (can be read responsively)

Time of Prayer: Ask participants to share joys and concerns. Pray for those concerns and pray with a special emphasis on creation care and being good stewards.

Closing Song: "He's Got the Whole World in His Hands"

Note: The planning team may want to invite a guest speaker who is actively working for faith-based eco-justice. This person could give a short message during your worship time and then participate in your station rotations, ideally facilitating Station 2. This person could also join your group for the fellowship time, either staffing an information table or informally networking with participants.

Faith Stations

Station 1. Creation Story–It Was Good

What You'll Need

Volunteer: station host

Sheet of black poster board

Sheet of white poster board

Sheet of light blue poster board

Yellow poster board cutouts of the sun, moon, and stars

Sheet of green poster board

Sheet of dark blue poster board

Pictures of plants, fish, and birds, and animals cut out from magazines and mounted on 3 separate sheets of poster board

Map of the United States, approximately 2' x 3' (ideally drawn freehand on a sheet of mural paper, including state outlines, or prepurchased)

Yarn

Scissors

Sticky notes

Markers

Pens

The host should welcome participants and ask them to gather in a semicircle. Explain that the group will be hearing and seeing the Creation story (Genesis 1:1-31). Tell the Creation story, inviting different volunteers to come up and hold the day and night (black and white poster board); the sky and water (light and dark blue poster board); the land and plants (green poster board and plant pictures poster); the sun, moon, and stars cutouts; the birds and fish poster; and the animals poster. When you get to the creation of people, invite a few volunteers to come up and be themselves!

During the story, emphasize God's words "It is good" by encouraging participants to say the phrase out loud with you. You should also emphasize verses 28-31, making the point that God entrusted his creation to us, his children. After the story, ask people to form small groups to answer the following questions:

1. What is your favorite part of God's creation?

2. What do you think God would say about how people are caring for his creation?

3. What is one thing you think God would like you to change about how you care for creation? (How can you take better care of God's creation?)

When groups are done, they can check out the wall map of the United States. Ask participants to mark their favorite local, county, state, and national parks across the country. They can write their last name and the park name right on the map. If using a smaller printed map, ask participants to mark the map with an X and then tape a piece of string to the X and run it off the map and tape it to the wall. Next to the end point, they can place a sticky note and write their name and the park name. If you have time remaining, ask each person to share one of her or his choices with the group.

Station 2. The Creation Team

What You'll Need

Volunteer: station host

Old white or light-colored T-shirts brought by participants

Earth-friendly fabric paint (mustard, grape juice, tomato or beet juice)

Assorted sizes of foam brushes

Bowls to hold the fabric paint

Newsprint for tables

2 large sheets of mural paper with 5 columns drawn on each with the headings *Home, Church, School, Town,* and *Planet*

Markers

Plastic grocery bags

Note: If the planning team is opposed to using this limited quantity of food as earth-friendly fabric paint, purchase nontoxic spray-on tie-dye paints from a craft store and follow the package directions.

Ahead of time, this station should be set up with long tables covered in a thick layer of newspaper. The host should welcome participants to the station and explain that all of God's children around the globe should be working as a team to help care for creation. In this session, participants will be identifying the things they do now to care for creation, as well as make plans to do more. They will also be making team shirts to show their unity of purpose.

First, lead a brainstorming session, asking the group about what they do now to care for creation. Write these answers in the related columns on the first mural sheet. You can also contribute suggestions or have handouts available with action information from the Christian environmental organizations listed at the beginning of this program.

After the brainstorming, participants can move to the team shirt activity. Participants will paint the old T-shirts they brought with them (have a supply of extra old shirts on hand for those who forget) with mustard and juices. They can make designs or write their names. The colors will fade after washing, but the stain of color will remain, reminding participants that no matter how careful we are with God's creation, we do leave our mark permanently. Our goal should be to leave things better than we found them.

Note: The shirts should be carefully rolled up and placed in a plastic bag for 24 hours after painting. Then they should be washed in cold water with 2 cups of vinegar. They can be washed in cold water with gentle detergent after that and hung dry or dried on low in the dryer. (See www.forallgenerations.com for pictures.)

April | Trees of Righteousness

Celebrate Arbor Day with a tree-planting project for all generations! Arbor Day is traditionally the fourth Friday in April; however, many southern and western states use alternate dates that are better suited for tree planting. Visit www.arborday.org/index.cfm for more information. Or visit www.edenprojects.org for community-based ideas that support responsible reforestation and long-term solutions to environmental destruction by the group Eden Reforestation Projects.

Alternatively, you might tie in a tree-planting activity with your Earth Day program (see pages 32–35 in this book), or use your Earth Day program to sign up volunteers to plant trees on a different day. Earth Day is held on April 22.

As participants paint, encourage them to continue to share ideas with one another about ways they can help care for creation. Throw out trivia and action facts from the Christian eco-justice material to stimulate discussion. As participants finish the shirts and before they leave, they should write on the second mural paper at least one action per person that can be taken as a "next step" in caring for creation.

Station 3. Recycled Scripture Sculptures

What You'll Need

Volunteers: station host

Recycled sculpture materials (all items should be rinsed, cleaned, and dried before using—pop cans, yogurt and pudding containers, assorted boxes, egg cartons, oatmeal tubs, lunch meat tubs, plastic bottle caps, old buttons, fabric and trim scraps, paper scraps, old magazines, greeting cards, and calendars, etc.)

Craft glue or hot glue

Markers

List of creation Scriptures (Leviticus 26:3-4, 6; Job 12:7-10; Psalm 96:10, 12; Psalm 104:25, 30; Isaiah 55:12-13; Ezekiel 34:17, 18)

Bibles

This station should be set up with long tables. The sculpture material, Bibles, and Scripture list should be set out at a central supply table. The other tables should be covered with newsprint and used as worktables. Participants can gather their supplies and bring them to the worktables.

The station host should welcome the participants to the sculpture station and invite groups to take a Scripture list and a Bible and find a place to read through the verses and choose one for their sculpture. After they have chosen a verse, they can create a sculpture that represents God's creation. They can use any of the materials on the supply table. If you have older couples or single adults, encourage them to work with a family group or partner with a child or two from a larger family. Or they can make their own individual sculptures to take home, as well.

Note: The selected verse should be written on paper and mounted on the sculpture.

Fellowship

Ideally this program should close with a time of fellowship; however, your planning team will need to decide how you want your event to flow. Consider serving organic fruits and vegetables or other organic treats (cheese, crackers, yogurt, etc.). If you live in a warmer climate and people's gardens are already producing, your team could ask for donations of home-grown items. Or, if serving a meal, think about making a vegetable soup where everyone brings one item from home to add to the soup (the planning team may want to choose a basic vegetable soup recipe and assign ingredients ahead of time). Either way, each event can be tailored to your group's needs and time constraints. Just be sure to include a time of fellowship in your program, whether a full meal or light refreshments.

CHAPTER 10

May
Mother's Day

Leader Background

Although motherhood celebrations and festivals can be found in ancient cultures dating back thousands of years, Mother's Day in the United States started with Julia Ward Howe's proclamation in 1870 to honor peace and motherhood. By 1873 June 2 was recognized as Mother's Day; however, the holiday did not gain recognition nationwide. Another follower of Howe, Anna Reeves Jarvis, along with her West Virginia women's group, began a tradition of Mother's Friendship Day to try to restore relationships destroyed by the Civil War. After her death, her daughter, Anna M. Jarvis, campaigned to create an official national Mother's Day. Her efforts started in her local church, Andrews Methodist Episcopal in Grafton, West Virginia, in 1908. Jarvis provided white carnations, her mother's favorite flower, to all worshipers. Today white carnations are traditionally given in honor of mothers who have died, while pink and red carnations are given in honor of living mothers. In 1914 President Woodrow Wilson affirmed Jarvis's hard work by declaring Mother's Day a United States holiday celebrated on the second Sunday in May.

Note: The planning team should keep in mind the faith-based focus of this celebration of mothers so that it becomes more than just a commercial holiday observance. In addition, the team should be aware that not everyone has a good relationship with his or her own mother, and you cannot assume that all participants joyfully celebrate the holiday or understand the heavenly parenting model that is being presented.

Program Focus: Models of motherhood from the Bible and beyond

Key Verses: "And Mary said, 'My soul magnifies the Lord, and my spirit rejoices in God my Savior, for he has looked with favor on the lowliness of his servant'" (Luke 1:46-48 NRSV).

Purpose:
a. To introduce/reintroduce famous mothers in the Bible: Sarai/Sarah, Jochebed, Naomi, Hannah, Mary, Elizabeth, Lydia
b. To give thanks for mothers everywhere
c. To explore ways that God is like a mother to us

Worship

Opening Song(s): Open your time together with 3–5 songs of praise and worship that support the theme of motherhood and parenting. Possibilities include "All Creatures of Our God and King," "For the Beauty of the Earth," "Near to the Heart of God," "Take My Life and Let It Be," "Honor Your Father and Mother," "Honor Your Parents," "Parents' Prayer."

Scripture Reading: Psalm 127

Time of Prayer: Ask participants to lift up the names of mothers for whom they give thanks or seek God's blessing.

Closing Song: "Love Divine, All Loves Excelling" or "Thank You for Hearing Me"

Faith Stations

Station 1. Mother Roots

What You'll Need

Volunteers: station host; 7 storytellers/actresses for each of the 6 passages (Sarah's story in Genesis 17:15-22 and 18:1-15; Jochebed's story in Exodus 2:1-10; Naomi's story in Ruth 1; Hannah's story in 1 Samuel 1:1-22; Mary's and Elizabeth's stories in Luke 1:26-56; Lydia's story in Acts 16:11-15)
Bible-time costumes (robes, tunics, etc.)
Flip chart/whiteboard and markers

There are two ways to facilitate this station. The easiest way is to recruit 7 women to play the 7 biblical mothers. Each woman will need a costume, and most will need a baby doll to hold. They should all be familiar enough with their story to be able to tell it conversationally (see passages above). The host can introduce each mother and give her 2–3 minutes to briefly tell her story.

For example: Jochebed (Moses' mother) would say something like:

Hello, brothers and sisters. I am the mother of Moses. You know Moses, don't you? He led God's people (the Israelites) out of slavery in Egypt, across the Red Sea, and into the wilderness, where God took care of us for 40 years. Life in Egypt was hard, and when I was pregnant with Moses, the ruler declared that all Israelite boy babies should be killed at birth. I was very scared for my son. I prayed that God would help us. After my son was born, I hid him for three months. When he got too big to hide in our home, I had my daughter place him in a basket and take him down to the Nile River where the Egyptian princess liked to bathe. My daughter hid Moses' basket in the water plants and then waited for the princess to discover my Moses in the basket. Soon she did, and she commanded her maids to bring my baby to her. The princess wanted to take Moses home, but she needed a woman to help care for him. My daughter came out of hiding and told the princess she knew a woman who could help. That woman was me! So I raised Moses from a baby to a little boy when he was old enough to join the princess at the palace. I trusted God to love and protect my family and me, and he did—in the most amazing way. Praise God!

The other way to facilitate this station is to have the station host serve as a third person narrator and bring up audience volunteers to symbolize the different women as the host tells their stories (similar to text above).

After the storytelling, the host should facilitate a discussion with the group and list ways that mothers care for their children and ways that God cares for his children, pointing out how these ways are very similar.

Station 2. Worship Banner

What You'll Need

Volunteer: station host

8' section of burlap, canvas, or felt for banner background

Felt or other fabric to make flowers for the banner

Permanent markers

Craft glue or hot glue

Picture books about mothers and Mother's Day

Anita Renfroe: Total MomSense DVD and TV/DVD player (optional)

This station should be set up with long worktables. The host should welcome participants to the station and explain that participants will all be helping to create a banner to use in your church's Mother's Day service. Participants can use any of the fabric supplies to create flowers to glue onto the banner. Somewhere on the flowers participants should put the names of the mothers they know and love and want to honor. (These don't have to be their own mothers and may be multiple flowers/names.)

May | Cinco de Mayo

Historically Cinco de Mayo celebrates the unlikely victory of the Mexican army over French invaders. Consider hosting a Cinco de Mayo celebration that connects this event in Mexican history to another unlikely victory in biblical history. Have a storyteller recreate the story of Joshua and the battle of Jericho by involving participants as Joshua's trumpet-blowing army. Then read a nonfiction picture book about the Battle of Puebla on May 5, 1862. Discuss the similarities. Other stations can include making paper towel tube trumpets and Mexican maracas and learning simple Cinco de Mayo songs, along with playing traditional Mexican party games and breaking a piñata (see sample program at www.forallgenerations.com).

When participants are done with the craft, they can find a book to read from what your team has supplied. You may also want to supply a copy of the DVD *Anita Renfroe: Total MomSense* and show the "What a Mom Says in a 24-Hour Period" clip (3 minutes).

Station 3. Games

What You'll Need

Volunteer: station host

You will need a large area for this station, either outside or in a gym or fellowship hall. The host should welcome participants and explain that the group will be playing some games that illustrate the nature of our relationship with God. The Bible teaches us that God is a loving parent to us. That means that, as with our earthly parents, we need to follow God's instructions, we need to work as a team with our brothers and sisters in Christ, and we need to joyfully celebrate our family connection. Sometimes when life gets hard or confusing, we forget that God is always the loving parent, even when he needs to discipline us and remind us to follow his Word. These games will help us get to know God as our parent. Play each game for about 10 minutes.

Mother May I?

For the game Mother May I? the host selects one person to be "Mother." The other participants all line up at the opposite end of the playing area. One at a time each participant asks "Mother" if she or he may take a different kind of step toward her. These steps can be as silly or as creative as the player wants (baby steps, giant steps, monkey-arm steps, jumping jack steps, hopping steps, chicken-flap steps, etc.). "Mother" then considers the request and gives her response, (yes, with a set number of steps; yes, with an alternative type/number of steps; or no). The participant obeys the directions and moves forward (or backward). The first person to tag "Mother" becomes the new "Mother." The host should explain that the purpose is to understand that when we see God as our parent, following God's instructions becomes a natural part of our relationship with him. He cares for us and is looking out for us.

Amoeba Race

Divide into teams of 8–10 people. Form circles by standing close together and facing outward. Join hands. The host can set up an obstacle course with points for the amoebas to navigate around. Amoebas cannot let go of hands and must remain standing side by side as they move through the course. Teams can also reconfigure for a second round and divide teams by similar height. When playing this way, link arms to make the contact tighter and movement more challenging. The host should explain that the purpose is to show that teamwork is necessary to get through life. God asks us to be part of the family of God and to work side by side with all his children.

Ha

The third game is a variation of the classic Ha. The group should stand or sit in a circle and place an arm around the shoulders of the persons next to them. The first person says "Ha." The second person says, "Ha ha." The third person says, "Ha ha ha." Continue with each subsequent person, adding one "ha" to what is said. If the person does not say the correct number of ha's, start over with the next person in line. Usually groups can only get to 4 or 5 ha's before the whole group begins to giggle and the game must restart. The host should explain that the purpose is to remind people that joy is part of our family connection with God. Remember to laugh and enjoy God and the blessings he gives his children.

Fellowship

Ideally this program should close with a time of fellowship. Your planning team, if doing advance sign up, may want to contact all of the "mothers" who plan on attending and ask for their three favorite foods. The team can then choose a refreshment/dinner menu that includes some or all of the favorites. Or, if the church has ever published a church cookbook, the team could choose to prepare some of the favorite recipes submitted by the moms of the church. In any case, each event can be tailored to your group's needs and time constraints. Just be sure to include a time of fellowship in your program, whether a full meal or light refreshments.

May | Teacher Appreciation Week

Typically observed during in the first full week of May, Teacher Appreciation Week offers all generations the opportunity to remember and celebrate those who have taught us—in Sunday school or Bible study, in elementary or high school, in sports or the arts, formally and informally.

• **Thank-You Note.** Write a thank-you note to your favorite teacher. Highlight something specific that he or she taught you that made a difference in your life.

• **Letter to the Editor.** Write a letter to the editor of your local newspaper thanking a specific teacher for making a difference in your life or your child's life.

• **Top Teacher.** Invite students (youth and adults) from your congregation to nominate their favorite Sunday school teacher and list three reasons why this teacher is fantastic. Draw names out of a hat or have a team review the nominees and vote on the top three or five. Award small appreciation gifts like Christian bookstore gift cards to the winning teachers, presented on behalf of the student and in honor of the teacher.

CHAPTER 11

May
Peacemaking

Program Focus: Peacemakers for God

Key Verse: "'Blessed are the peacemakers, for they will be called children of God'" (Matthew 5:9 NRSV).

Purpose:
a. To identify peacemakers in this world and in the Bible
b. To explore what it means to be a peacemaker for God
c. To plan a "next step" in becoming a peacemaker for God

Leader Background

In Matthew 5:9 Jesus tells his listeners, "Blessed are the peacemakers, for they will be called children of God" (NRSV). Peacemaking is not an "out there" concept reserved for world leaders; peacemaking is a personal project. Peacemaking is part of being reconciled to God and takes place on several levels—in our homes, in our churches, in our local communities, and in communities around the globe. While individually none of us can solve the world's hurts, we can, individually, do our part to be peacemakers wherever God has placed us.

Worship

Opening Song(s): Open your time together with 3–5 songs of praise and worship that support the theme of peacemaking. Possibilities include "A Mighty Fortress," "All People That on Earth Do Dwell," "There Is a Balm in Gilead," "Let the Peace of God Reign," "Peace Like a River," "Let There Be Peace on Earth."

Scripture Reading: Psalm 85:8-13 (read responsively; after each verse read by the leader, the people respond, "Amen. Let it be.")

Time of Prayer: Ask participants to lift up situations needing reconciliation and peace. Pray with an emphasis on seeking and finding reconciliation with God so that we can serve as peacemakers in the world.

Closing Song: "Dona Nobis Pacem" or "Go Now in Peace"

Faith Stations

Station 1. Peacemaker Role Models

What You'll Need

Volunteers: station host, storyteller to play Laban and Esau

Bible-time costumes (robes, tunics, etc.)

20 small landscaping stones to form the "heap of witness"

The host will tell the story of Jacob and Laban making peace, followed shortly by Jacob making peace with his brother, Esau, from whom he stole the blessing and birthright honors when they were younger. The host should be very familiar with the text (Genesis 31–33) so that she or he is comfortable telling the story in character as Jacob. The other storyteller will prepare the same text to be the character of Laban and then Esau. The host can call up volunteers to serve as other characters in the story (e.g., Laban goes into the tents of Jacob and his family searching for his idols, which he thinks have been stolen by Jacob). Volunteers can serve as Leah, the two maids, and Rachel and shrug their shoulders and indicate they have nothing to hide. They can also, at Jacob's direction, gather the stones and place them in a heap.

After the story, the host should ask participants to get into groups of 6–10 people to discuss the following questions:

1. In the first part of the story, Laban takes the lead peacemaker role, extending the hand of peace to his son-in-law, Jacob. How does this help Jacob when he meets his brother, Esau?

2. What other biblical peacemakers can you name? What did they do to work for peace?

3. Who are some famous (or not so famous) peacemakers who have worked to bring peace between people or nations? Why do you think they are good peacemaker role models?

After 15 or so minutes of discussion, the host can wrap up this station by asking groups to share a few names from questions 2 and 3.

May | Asian-Pacific American Month

Originally designated as a commemorative week by President Jimmy Carter, Asian-Pacific American month was signed into law by President George H. W. Bush in 1992 and seeks to recognize the contributions of Asians and Pacific Islanders in the history and culture of the United States. For more ideas and background information, visit asianpacificheritage.gov/ or www.smithsonianeducation.org/educators/resource_library/asian_american_resources.html.

• **Asian-Pacific Cook-off.** Explore Asian-Pacific culture by hosting an intergenerational cooking night. Bring in volunteers familiar with Asian-Pacific recipes to teach participants how to prepare various dishes. Eat the class projects for dinner! Ask a volunteer chef also to teach the group to say grace in his or her native language.

• **Getting to Know You.** Utilizing your church's denominational/organizational office or personal contacts, invite a diverse group of Asian-Pacific people to come share their culture with your congregation. Set up stations that involve storytelling with folktales and fables, traditional music and dance, and traditional arts and crafts. Also ask these guests to share their faith experiences in their native country or in an ethnic church setting, or have them read familiar Bible stories in their native languages.

Station 2. Peace Path

What You'll Need

Volunteer: station host,

Peace Path map that shows participants a course
to follow

Peace Path course marked out inside/outside
your church

Note: The path can be set up inside your church using multiple rooms or outside on your grounds or a mix of both. Have 6 to 8 stops set up. These stations can provide a Scripture verse to read with a prayer theme or require some kind of action by participants.

The host should welcome participants and hand out the maps. (See suggested activities below.) Explain that participants will be traveling the path and stopping at the different stations to engage in peacemaking activities. Groups may visit the stations in any order. They should remain fairly quiet, as many of these activities involve prayer or reflection.

May | National Day of Prayer

Every year on the first Thursday in May, people of faith around the United States hold vigils or special worship services in honor of the National Day of Prayer. Consider how you might involve all generations in your church or community in such an observance.

• **Prayer Breakfast.** Join with other churches to host a prayer breakfast or dinner with opportunities for silent personal and spoken group prayer, as well as prayers led by children and adults.

• **Prayer Labyrinth.** Create a prayer labyrinth (either permanent or temporary) with meditation stations. Invite both the congregation and the public to come walk the labyrinth. (See www.forallgenerations.com for additional details.)

Note: Depending on the activities your planning team includes along the path, you may need to collect assorted supplies (such as Bibles, pens, index cards, building blocks, etc.) and have those set out at the stops.

Sample Peace Path

Stop 1. Read Matthew 5:9. Why do you think being a peacemaker makes you a child of God? Discuss with your group. Have someone in your group pray that you will act as peacemakers and children of God.

Stop 2. Read Isaiah 11:1-9. This passage is often referred to as the "Peaceable Kingdom." What do you think Isaiah is telling us can happen because of Jesus (the shoot from the stump of Jesse)? Discuss with your group. Pray that God will use you to work for peace among people who are at odds with one another.

Stop 3. Read Ephesians 4:1-6. If we are all one in the Spirit of God, why can't we get along? Which of these is hardest for you to do—be humble, be gentle and kind, be patient, be understanding? Discuss with your group. Have someone pray that God will help you live the life worthy of the one to which he has called you, one that is joined to others in unity and peace.

Stop 4. Read Ephesians 2:13-19. Together we build up the dwelling place for God. Think about one thing you can do to work for peace in this world and help build the dwelling place for God. Go around your group and have each person lay down a block to make a symbolic house for God. As you lay down the block, name the one thing you are going to do to work for peace.

Stop 5. Read John 14:25-27. Jesus left us his peace as a promise of good things to come. What things worry you? Discuss with your group. Then have someone pray that Jesus' peace will comfort you and encourage you even when life feels scary and difficult.

Stop 6. Read Colossians 3:12-17. Paul tells us that forgiveness is part of being a peacemaker. Think of a person you may have hurt with your words or actions. Have you apologized and asked for forgiveness from this person? Peacemaking is hard work. It takes time to rebuild relationships, but Jesus asks us to be peacemakers and let his peace rule in our hearts and guide our steps. If you are willing, share the name of the person you've been thinking about. Then have someone pray for your group that the peace of Christ will rule your words and actions and that you will be able to mend broken relationships and work for peace in your life and in the world.

Station 3. Give Peace a Chance

What You'll Need

Volunteer: station host

Copies of peace sign handout

Pens/markers

Peacemaker picture book biographies

Background research on peacemakers (see Note)

Flip chart/whiteboard and markers

Note: The peace sign handout is simply a circle drawn on an 8¹/2" x 11" piece of paper and divided with a Y to form a peace sign. In one section write, "Family"; in the second section write, "Church/ School/Work"; and in the third section write, "Community/World." Make one copy for each person. It will also be helpful for the planning team or station host to have done background research on famous peacemakers. To get started, visit http://www.almaz .com/nobel/peace/peace.html (a list of all Nobel Peace Prize winners) or http://www.salsa.net/peace/faces/ (a large selection of international peacemakers, each with a short bio and pictures, sponsored by the San Antonio peaceCENTER in Texas). Finally, after the team has come up with a list of 8–10 famous peacemakers, use your local library to find picture book biographies on these individuals and have them available for reading at this station or print articles and pictures from your Internet research.

The host should welcome participants and ask them to gather in a semicircle. Lead a brainstorming discussion about peacemaker qualities and write these on a flip chart/whiteboard. Ask the group to name places in their lives where they see peacemakers at work and list those situations/people.

Participants can then move to worktables to complete the peace sign handout and/or move around the room and read the peacemaker picture book biographies and/or famous peacemakers info if your planning team is making that available. Explain that the handout asks participants to think of one peacemaker quality they demonstrate at home and one quality they demonstrate (or would like to demonstrate) at school/church/work. For the third section (community/world), participants should think of a "next step" they can take to be a peacemaker on this more public level. Younger children can draw pictures in the spaces (being kind to a friend in need, patiently listening to a sibling's problem or solving a sibling's problem, etc.).

Fellowship

Ideally this program should close with a time of fellowship. Consider serving cookies decorated with peace signs or dove-shaped cookies. Or, if offering a full meal, the planning team may choose to serve foods from countries where war, poverty, and/or famine is ongoing and peace is a challenge. If choosing this meal option, the team might also display a world map and highlight these areas of the world that are in conflict or affected by mass poverty and famine so that participants can better identify with global areas in need of peace and healing. Either way, each event can be tailored to your group's needs and time constraints. Just be sure to include a time of fellowship in your program, whether a full meal or light refreshments.

CHAPTER 12

May
Pentecost

Leader Background

In Malcolm Shotwell's book *Creative Programs for Churches* (Judson Press, 1985), he describes Pentecost in this way:

> It has been said that Christmas is the Festival of Love; Good Friday, the Festival of Mercy; Easter, the Festival of Life; and Pentecost, the Festival of Power. "But you will receive power when the Holy Spirit comes on you; and you will be my witnesses in Jerusalem, and in all Judea and Samaria, and to the ends of the earth" (Acts 1:8 NIV). This prophecy of Jesus needs to be preached and put into practice today as much as it was in the first century. In fact, the Holy Spirit is the power source, the supply department for the energy that will keep the church alive and aglow all year! (p. 38)

Pentecost means "fiftieth" and falls on the seventh Sunday after Easter. It celebrates the birth of the Christian church, as the Holy Spirit came and filled the new believers with the power to go out and make disciples of all the nations.

Worship

Opening Song(s): Open your time together with 3–5 songs of praise and worship that support the theme of serving Jesus and serving others. Possibilities include "Blessing and Honor and Glory and Power," "Come, You People, Rise and Sing," "God of Grace and God of Glory," "Spirit of the Living God," "As We Gather," "Let the Fire Fall."

Scripture Reading: John 15:5-15

Time of Prayer: Ask participants to lift up joys and concerns for your local church and the global church. The leader should pray for all churches who love and serve God.

Closing Song: "Ancient of Days"

Program Focus: The birth of the Christian church

Key Verse: "And suddenly from heaven there came a sound like the rush of
a violent wind, and it filled the entire house where they were sitting" (Acts 2:2 NRSV).

Purpose:
a. To introduce/reintroduce the story of the birth of the church
b. To celebrate the presence of the Holy Spirit in our lives
c. To explore the original model of "church" and connect it to present practices of worship, study, and fellowship

Faith Stations

Station 1. The Birth of the Church

What You'll Need

Volunteers: station host, props assistant
Large electric fan
Foreign language CDs
CD players
Paper
Pens

The host will be telling the story of the birth of the church, so she or he should be very familiar with Acts 2. The props assistant will turn on the fan when cued by the host. The assistant will also turn on the various CD players so that participants hear many different languages being spoken/sung all at once (doesn't matter what is being said, just that there are many languages being spoken). The host can continue reading through Peter's sermon and the first gathering and fellowship of the early believers.

After the story, the host should ask participants to get into groups of 6–10 people to discuss the following questions (give each group a sheet of paper and a pen to record their answers):

1. How do you think the people felt when the Holy Spirit came through the room?

2. What did Peter say they needed to do? (Repent and be baptized since they all were Jewish. Technically the church didn't exist until the Holy Spirit filled the first believers.)

3. How are these first believers models for us today? What did they do to live out their new faith?

4. Make a list of ways that you live out your faith. How do you compare to the first believers?

After 10–15 minutes of discussion, the host can wrap up this station by asking groups to share a few answers from question 4.

Station 2. Power Pinwheel

What You'll Need

Volunteer: station host
Pinwheel supplies (will vary)

Note: Pinwheel craft kits can be ordered online from school supply companies. Search for "balsa wood pinwheel kits." Some companies offer craft-foam based kits, but these will make pinwheels that will be too heavy to be blown. Approximate cost is $1 per pinwheel, so you will need to budget accordingly and/or charge a small fee to cover these station expenses.

The host should welcome participants and explain that they will be making pinwheels to symbolize the powerful wind of the Holy Spirit that breathed life into the first church. Pinwheel kits should contain all necessary supplies. On a whiteboard/chalk board, write, "Suddenly a sound like the blowing of a violent wind came from heaven and filled the whole house where they were sitting" (Acts 2:2 NIV). Participants can include this Bible verse when decorating their pinwheels.

If you have time left after the pinwheels are finished, organize contests to see whose pinwheel spins the longest on one breath of air or do a relay where two teams compete to have the longest spinning chain. With the host timing, the first person on each team blows her or his pinwheel. Only when it stops may the next person blow her or his. Continue on to the end of the line. The host will compare final times.

Station 3. Birthday Party Prep

What You'll Need

Volunteer: station host

Game and snack supplies per your planning team

5¹/₂" x 8¹/₂" sheets of colored construction paper

Stick-on bows

Markers

Drawing/enlarged photo/model of your church

Sticky gift tag labels

The host should welcome participants and ask them to gather at worktables. Their first task is to think of a gift each person can give the church to help it grow—for example, money, a specific volunteer service, or invitations to others to attend worship or fellowship programs. Whatever it is, each person should write it down or draw a picture of it on a sheet of construction paper. Then he or she can attach a sticky gift tag label addressed to your church and given by (insert name), along with a sticky bow. "Gifts" can be placed on a table near the drawing/photo/model of your church so that people can view all the gifts that are being given.

When participants are done with this first step, the host, with the help of the kitchen crew, can engage them in food prep for the birthday party (decorating cakes/cookies, making punch, creating snacks, etc.) and/or playing a few party games, according to how your planning team would like to run the fellowship–birthday party portion of the program. Great theme games include anything with air/balloons, such as balloon relay races in which teams have to blow an inflated balloon down a course and back or run in pairs race down and back with a balloon in between their backs. Balloon volleyball involves teams sitting on the floor on opposite sides of a 12' length of rope tied to two chairs. Without taking their bottoms off the floor, they must "serve" the balloon over the net. If it touches the floor on the opposite side, the serving team scores a point. This can also be played seated on chairs.

Fellowship

The birthday party for the church will take place during the fellowship time, either as a full dinner or dessert only. Your planning team may also want to play music and have other party games going on. Decide what will work best for your congregation and time frame.

Note: An additional party option might be to do a musical celebration after the food has been served. Malcolm Shotwell calls this a "Festival of Power" in his *Creative Programs for Churches* book and says, "Let this birthday party be a time to review the entire season of worship through music. Include in your festival times for praise and thanksgiving for the church—past, present, and future" (p. 39). If this is going to be an interactive sing-along format, the planning team may want to solicit input from the congregation a month before the event to get a list of favorite hymns/praise songs and have those lyrics/music available at the party.

CHAPTER 13

June
Father's Day

Leader Background

Unlike Mother's Day, which has long and involved historical and spiritual roots, Father's Day emerged in the early part of the twentieth century. Originally conceived by two women, the holiday got the nod from President Calvin Coolidge in 1924, although the third Sunday in June wasn't set as Father's Day until President Lyndon Johnson's action in 1966. It wasn't until 1972 that President Richard Nixon declared Father's Day an official national holiday. While the carnation is the official Mother's Day flower, the rose is used on Father's Day, with red roses given to fathers who are living and white roses given out for fathers who have died.

Note: The planning team should keep in mind the faith-based focus of this celebration of fathers so that it becomes more than just a commercial holiday observance. In addition, the team should be aware that not everyone has a good relationship with his or her own father, and you cannot assume that all participants joyfully celebrate the holiday or understand the heavenly parenting model that is being presented.

Program Focus: Models of fatherhood from the Bible and beyond

Key Verse: "Because you are children, God has sent the Spirit of his Son into our hearts, crying, 'Abba! Father!'" (Galatians 4:6 NRSV).

Purpose:
a. To introduce/reintroduce famous fathers in the Bible: Abraham, Jacob, Laban, and Joseph
b. To give thanks for fathers everywhere
c. To explore ways that God is like a father to us

Worship

Opening Song(s): Open your time together with 3–5 songs of praise and worship that support the theme of God our Father and parenting. Possibilities include "Faith of Our Fathers," "How Firm a Foundation," "In Christ Alone," "For the Beauty of the Earth," "Glorify Thy Name," "As for Me and My House," "Awesome God," "Give Us Clean Hands."

Scripture Reading: Galatians 4:1-7

Time of Prayer: Invite participants to lift up names of fathers or men who have been like fathers to them and give thanks or ask for continued blessing or healing. Offer prayers with an emphasis on our Father God setting the example for our earthly fathers and giving thanks for men who model godly behavior.

Closing Song: "Father, We Adore You"

Faith Stations

Station 1. Abraham: A Model of Loyal Faith

What You'll Need

Volunteer: station host

Bible-time costume

Sand art craft supplies (buy sand art kits that include plastic containers and multiple colors of sand, or collect baby food jars with lids and purchase only the multiple colors of sand; you will also need bowls for sand, spoons, and newsprint to cover tables)

Small paper plates

Craft paint and thin brushes

Permanent-colored markers

Small sticky-back foam stars

Craft glue

The host should welcome participants and invite them to sit in a semicircle. You will be telling the story of God's promise (the Abrahamic covenant) to Abraham to make his descendants more numerous than the grains of sand in the desert or stars in the sky, so you should be familiar with Genesis 15–17 and 21–22. These chapters tell the story of how an old and childless Abraham is promised a son by God,

how Abraham and Sarah take matters into their own hands when they don't think God's timetable is working, and how God fulfills his promise to make Abraham a father. Just as children need to learn to obey their parents, Abraham needed to learn to be obedient to God, his heavenly Father, but he did demonstrate his faithfulness and loyalty to God.

Note: This story has some scary elements in it for young children as Abraham follows God's instructions to sacrifice Isaac, the son he had been waiting for. God stops Abraham from actually killing Isaac and provides a ram to offer as a sacrifice. Still, this will be frightening for young children (and adults, as well) to think that Abraham heard a voice from heaven telling him to sacrifice his son and that he was going to do so. The storyteller should be careful to explain that God does not regularly speak to fathers, telling them to sacrifice their children, and that God was testing Abraham's faith because Abraham had been disobedient to God in the birth of his first son, Ishmael. There are many times when we cannot possibly know what God was thinking or why he chose to act in a certain way, but the bottom line is that Abraham had not trusted God's timetable or God's promise of children and tried to adjust God's plan. The focus in the story should be on Abraham's faith, disobedience, and then return to faithful obedience to God his Father.

After the story, lead the group in singing the children's song "Father Abraham." Then invite participants to move to worktables to create the sand and star project. Each newsprint-covered table should hold the following supplies: one jar or container for each person, bowls of colored sand with spoons for filling jars, paint and brushes or permanent markers, sticky-back foam stars, and a few bottles of craft glue.

Each participant should first decorate a jar lid by painting it a dark color, letting it dry, and then painting stars on it, or by coloring a lid with permanent marker and placing sticky-back foam stars on it. The jar can then be filled by layering different colors of sand. When the jar is completely filled, the participant should run a line of glue around the inside lip of the lid and screw the cap into place.

Station 2. Joseph: A Model of Humble Faith

What You'll Need

Volunteer: station host

Bible-time costume

Recording of "Who Am I?" by Casting Crowns

Laptop computer/projector/screen/Internet access to YouTube for worship video of "Who Am I?" (optional)

Assorted scrap wood

Sandpaper

Hammers

Nails

Newsprint to cover tables

The host should welcome participants and ask them to gather in a semicircle. You will be telling the story of Jesus' father Joseph, so you should be familiar with Matthew 1 and Luke 2:1-7. To start the story, either play a recording of the Casting Crowns song "Who Am I?" or select and show one of the many "Who Am I?" worship videos found on YouTube.com. This song is sung from Joseph's perspective as he struggles to figure out why God chose him to be Jesus' earthly father. What the song declares is that it is because of who God is and what God does that ordinary people can be used by God to do extraordinary things.

After the song, move right into telling Joseph's story. The focus should be on Joseph's good moral character and human decency, his initial reaction to the news of Mary's pregnancy, and how he submitted to God's will after the visit by the angel in his sleep. He continued to follow through with his earthly father duties, like taking his wife to Bethlehem for the census, because God expected him to be a responsible husband and father who followed the law and took care of his family. Joseph did not run around Bethlehem with a sign on his back that said, "Father to the Son of God." He humbly accepted his role as earthly father and did what was required of him.

After the story, direct participants over to the newsprint-covered worktables where each person can select 2 pieces of wood to make a cross. They can sand the wood edges to remove any potential splinters and then nail the pieces together. Adults should assist small children as needed.

Station 3. Laban, Esau, and Jacob: A Model of a Forgiving Faith

What You'll Need

Volunteer: station host

Bible-time costume

Sheets of sticky-back craft magnets cut into 3" hearts

Address labels preprinted with the Mizpah (Genesis 31:49)

Colored permanent markers

Scissors

The host should welcome participants and ask them to gather in a semicircle. The host will be telling Jacob's story so she or he should be familiar with Genesis 27–33. These chapters include background information on Jacob and how he stole the birthright and blessing from his brother, Esau, and how he came to know Laban, his uncle and father-in-law. The focus on the story will be taken from chapters Genesis 31–33. Jacob had taken his family and property and secretly moved away from Laban. Laban chased Jacob but forgave him for running away and taking his daughters and his property. Laban established a covenant to recognize their reconciliation. Jacob, who had often lied and schemed, perhaps realized for the first time the healing power of forgiveness from his father-in-law.

The second part of the story deals with Jacob's reunion and reconciliation with his brother, Esau, from whom he stole the family birthright. Jacob sought forgiveness from God for his sins against Esau and then approached Esau with a contrite heart and a willingness to restore their relationship. Jacob was a father who learned the value of forgiveness and healing broken relationships so that he might be more like his heavenly Father.

After the story, the host can direct participants to the worktables. On each table should be one heart magnet per person, one verse label per person, permanent markers, and scissors. The Mizpah magnets are made by putting the label on the heart and decorating the magnets with markers. The magnets can be cut into two pieces, as the Mizpah blessing is often shared between two friends, with each person taking a half of a locket bearing the verse. Similarly, participants can choose to give half of their magnet to a friend or family member.

Fellowship

Ideally this program should close with a time of fellowship. Like the Mother's Day fellowship option, the planning team may want to get some input from attending fathers on their favorite refreshments. Possibilities might include manly snacks like chips, nuts, and pretzels or a cook-out menu featuring burgers and hot dogs. However, each event can be tailored to your group's needs and time constraints. Just be sure to include a time of fellowship in your program, whether a full meal or light refreshments.

CHAPTER 14

June
Juneteenth

Leader Background

Although President Abraham Lincoln issued the Emancipation Proclamation on January 1, 1863, during the Civil War, not all slaves were immediately told of this executive order that granted them freedom. It wasn't until the last Union troop marched into Texas on June 19, 1865, two months after the official end to the war, that slavery formally ended. This day became known as Juneteenth and was celebrated as a holiday across the United States, mainly by African Americans but more recently by entire communities and states wanting to recognize this historic day.

However, the end of the war and the legal end of slavery didn't mean that all brokenness was mended. Relationships between Southern and Northern states and African Americans and whites had suffered terribly because of the war. Race relations are still a challenge for Americans today. Even with the work of Dr. Martin Luther King Jr. and other civil rights leaders over the past fifty years, much remains to be done. This program will allow participants to have conversations about slavery, freedom, and race relations in a safe environment and from a faith-based perspective.

Note: For additional information on Juneteenth, visit the official Juneteenth website at http://www.juneteenth.com.

Program Focus: Liberation and emancipation

Key Verse: "For whoever was called in the Lord as a slave is a freed person belonging to the Lord, just as whoever was free when called is a slave of Christ" (1 Corinthians 7:22 NRSV).

Purpose:

a. To learn about the historic significance of Juneteenth, when news of the Emancipation Proclamation finally reached Texas (the farthest flung slave state)

b. To explore issues of slavery, freedom, and race relations in the United States today

c. To connect historical issues of emancipation with spiritual lessons of freedom in Christ

Worship

Opening Song(s): Open your time together with 3–5 songs of praise and worship that support the theme of freedom. Possibilities include "God of Grace and God of Glory," "Mine Eyes Have Seen the Glory," "Go Down Moses," "Swing Low Sweet Chariot," "There Is a Balm in Gilead," "Pharaoh, Pharaoh."

Scripture Reading: Psalm 146 (can be read responsively, alternating verses)

Time of Prayer: Invite participants to share joys and concerns related to race relations in their local community or in the larger national and global settings. The leader can also pray with an emphasis on peace and reconciliation among all people.

Closing Song: "In Christ There Is No East or West" or "I Am Free"

Faith Stations

Station 1. Stories and Songs about Freedom

What You'll Need

Volunteer: station host
Picture books about the Civil War, the Underground Railroad, and Juneteenth
CDs of African American spirituals
CD player
Flip chart/poster board and markers

Note: If you have a space in your church with comfortable chairs and couches, use this area for this station. If not, make your station space as reader-friendly as possible with clusters of chairs grouped together around the room.

Have music playing as participants enter. The host should welcome participants and let them know this is an individually paced station. Explain that scattered around the room are books on Juneteenth, the Civil War, and the Underground Railroad. Groups can move about the room reading different books. Encourage adults to follow up the stories with questions such as, "How do you think the slaves felt on June 19? What about other Americans?" "How would you have felt if you were a traveler on the Underground Railroad?" After 20–25 minutes of reading, ask groups to share the title of the book(s) they read and one thing they learned from or enjoyed about the story. Write this information on the flip chart/poster board, along with their family name or initials. This reading list can be displayed during fellowship time to stimulate more conversation.

Station 2. The Bible's Freedom Story

What You'll Need

Volunteer: station host
Desert storytelling box (large, low-sided rectangular tub approximately 2' x 3', filled with a few inches of sand)
At least 2 4" action figures (1 for Moses and 1 for Pharaoh) converted into Bible people with a simple cloth tunic and tie belt, or make 4" characters out of poster board or cardboard and clothe with tunics and tie belts (see photos at www.forallgenerations.com)
Building blocks to make a pyramid
Small container of mud and straw
Plague items (river of blood: red and blue streamers; frogs: small green craft pompoms; gnats: tiny black craft pompoms; flies: very small black craft pompoms; dead cattle: plastic cows; boils: tiny red craft pompoms; hail: tiny white craft pompoms; locusts: very small brown craft pompoms; darkness: a black bath towel or piece of black cloth to cover the storytelling box)
2 long strips of blue cloth for the parting of the Red Sea
Bibles for the groups

Welcome participants and ask them to gather in a semicircle around the storytelling box. The host will tell the story of how the Israelites escaped from slavery, thanks to God, so she or he should be familiar with Exodus 2–14. Much of this will be background information and condensed for the listeners. Focus on the Israelites' difficult lives (including the fact that they lived in a culture where many false gods were worshiped), Moses' conversations with God and then with Pharaoh, the 10 plagues, and the escape from slavery in Egypt through the Red Sea.

Note: The storytelling box should have a pyramid built from blocks in one corner and a strip of blue streamers running the length of the box to symbolize the Nile River.

Before starting the story, ask a few questions to get people thinking about slavery, such as:

1. What is slavery?

2. What are some historical examples of slavery?

3. Why do you think people felt it was okay to own other people?

4. What happens to the relationships between people when one group owns another group?

5. Physical slavery is one kind of slavery, but we can also be slaves to things. What things do we let control us? (money, people's opinions, influential people, etc.)

As you tell the story, move the figures in the desert box and display different story elements (the mud-straw mix and the blocks that form the pyramid when describing the Israelites' life in slavery, the replacing of the blue streamers with red streamers when the river turns to blood, the scattering of green pompoms across the box for the plague of the frogs, etc.). To further involve participants in the story, ask for volunteers to scatter the "plagues" across the box.

After the story, hand out Bibles and ask participants to gather in small groups to finish the following statements and answer the question.

1. Life in Egypt was . . .

2. If I were a slave I would . . .

3. If I were Moses I would have . . .

4. If I were Pharaoh I would have . . .

5. The awful life of a slave is like our lives when we don't know Jesus. Jesus frees us from our sins and takes away those burdens. Have someone in your group read out loud 1 Corinthians 7:21-24. What do the Exodus story and these verses from 1 Corinthians tell us about God's view of slavery?

Station 3. Treating Others Differently

What You'll Need

Volunteer: station host
TV/DVD player
***Dr. Seuss' Animated Televised Classics: Green Eggs and Ham and Other Favorites* DVD for "The Sneetches" episode**
6 or 7 different colors of streamers cut into 36" strips (1 per person)

Note: You will need a large open space to play the first game.

The host should welcome participants and ask them each to take a streamer and tie it on their neck or arm or leg. Choose one person to be "It." "It" will make all the rules in this game of Color Tag. "It" will call out the color(s) that must be chased by the other colors. "It" should also choose one color to be the "Freers." If people wearing the chosen colors are tagged, they must freeze in place until a Freer runs by to unfreeze them. Freers can also be tagged and frozen. After a minute or so of play, the first person to be tagged becomes the new "It" and makes new rules. The host should facilitate this transition.

After participants have played the game for 5 to 10 minutes, gather the group around the TV/DVD player. Ask players how they felt when one person got to make all the rules and could prevent them from playing the whole time. Introduce the video by explaining that this Dr. Seuss story looks at what happens when one group thinks they are better than another group and makes rules that exclude some group members from certain activities. After viewing the DVD, ask participants to form small groups to answer the following questions:

1. How does the Sneetches' experience symbolize what happens in our own country among people of different skin colors, ethnic backgrounds, languages, or religions?

2. The Sneetches story has a happy ending. In the real world, we're still working on the happy ending. What is one thing you can do to work toward

treating everyone as equals regardless of their race, religion, ethnic background, etc.?

Once the groups have had 5–10 minutes for discussion, ask groups to share a few of their responses.

Fellowship

Ideally this program should close with a time of fellowship. Whether serving simple snacks or a full meal, the planning team may want to do some research on traditional African American foods (even better if you can find a local expert to help you plan and prepare!) and offer culturally themed refreshments. However, each event can be tailored to your group's needs and time constraints. Just be sure to include a time of fellowship in your program, whether a full meal or light refreshments.

CHAPTER 15

July
Independence Day

Program Focus: Celebrating our spiritual and personal freedoms

Key Verses: "'If you continue in my word, you are truly my disciples; and you will know the truth, and the truth will make you free'" (John 8:31-32 NRSV).

Purpose:
a. To explore the historical context for Independence Day in the United States
b. To explore ways that our faith in God frees us
c. To celebrate our spiritual and personal freedoms in our country

Leader Background

Independence Day in the United States recognizes the formal adoption of the Declaration of Independence by the Continental Congress, which until then had governed the thirteen colonies with British oversight. Although the Declaration wasn't officially signed until August 1776, July 4 is considered the day the Declaration was born and, as such, the holiday. The first city celebration was held in Philadelphia on July 8 of that year when the Declaration was read in public for the first time. Since then Americans have celebrated Independence Day with parades and picnics, even though Congress didn't make it an official paid, federal holiday until 1941.

Worship

Opening Song(s): Open your time together with 3–5 songs of praise and worship that support the theme of American independence, as well as freedom in Christ. Possibilities include "O Beautiful for Spacious Skies," "A Mighty Fortress," "My Country 'Tis of Thee," "In Christ Alone," "Holy Is the Lord," "Not to Us," and "You Are My All in All."

Scripture Reading: Galatians 5:1, 13-14; Ephesians 4:1-3

Time of Prayer: Invite participants to share joys and concerns related to America's independence and the freedoms we enjoy. The leader can also pray with an emphasis on the need to be spiritually free through Christ.

Closing Song: "In Christ There Is No East or West" or "I Am Free"

Faith Stations

Station 1. History in the Making

What You'll Need

Volunteer: station host

Picture books about the Declaration of Independence, the U.S. Constitution, colonial America, and the Revolutionary War (in particular, find a copy of *We the Kids* by David Catrow [Dial, 2002])

Copies of the text of the Declaration of Independence and the U.S. Constitution preamble

Flip chart/poster board and markers

Note: If you have a space in your church with comfortable chairs and couches, use this area for this station. If not, make your station space as reader-friendly as possible with clusters of chairs grouped around the room.

The host should welcome participants and gather them in a semicircle. Explain that in order to celebrate a piece of history, we must know why it is we're celebrating. Independence Day is when the United States of America declared itself to be a nation independent from England. The colonists wanted to establish a democratic government led by the people and for the people. They did not want to serve a greedy king who lived across the ocean. Read the first paragraph through the first sentence of the second paragraph of the Declaration of Independence (". . . life, liberty and the pursuit of happiness"). Then read *We the Kids* to the group, explaining that this book helps us understand the personal freedoms we have in this country as guaranteed by the U.S. Constitution. Historically, the Constitution came thirteen years after the Declaration of Independence, but it shares the same values of freedom and independence as the Declaration of Independence, which gave the United States its freedom from England.

After the host reads to the participants, they can move about the room and find other books to read in small groups. When participants have read for about fifteen minutes, gather them back and ask them to share the title and author of the book(s) they read and one thing they learned from or enjoyed about the story, and write them on a flip chart or sheet of poster board. Also ask the group to list freedoms they enjoy and are thankful for as Americans. This thankful list can be used during grace if serving a picnic meal.

Station 2. The Truth Shall Set You Free

What You'll Need

Volunteer: station host

Soft Nerf-type ball

List of Bible verses

Bible

Small sheets of paper and pencils for scorekeeping (optional)

Note: For this station, you will need a large, open space.

The host should welcome participants and ask them to gather in a circle. If there are more than 20 people at one time, break into groups of 10–20. Explain that this station will help participants understand Jesus' words in John about the truth. Jesus is described as the Way, the ruth, and the Life. If we know Jesus, we know the truth, and the truth will set us free from sin (the choices we make that do not honor God).

The first game is an exercise in knowing the truth. Each person needs to think of one truth and one lie about himself or herself. Adults can help children come up with these. Then, one at a time, participants should go around the circle telling the one truth and one lie. The others have to guess which statement is the truth. The group can shout out the answer, or the host can ask for a show of hands, and each player can keep score as to how many correct truth guesses he or she had.

When everyone has had a turn to guess, the host should ask the following questions:

1. How did you determine if the person was telling the truth or lying?

2. How do we determine what is the truth in the real world?

3. How does our friendship with Jesus help us figure out the truth?

4. Listen as I read from John 8:31-36. What do you think it means that the truth will set you free?

For the second game, the group will need to be in a large open space. Divide the group into pairs (child-adult pairs will work best). One team is chosen to be "It." They stand in the center. They are team number 1. The host then numbers the other teams. "It" has a list of true/false statements and a ball. "It" says, "Ready, set, go!" On "go" all the other pairs run while "It" tosses the ball in the air. As "It" catches the ball, "It" calls out one of the team numbers and everyone must freeze.

"It" then reads the first statement, and the pair must say if the statement is truth from the Bible or false wisdom from the world. If they choose correctly, that pair becomes the new "It." If they choose incorrectly, they are sent to "jail" and can only be freed by another team correctly answering a true statement (i.e., the truth will set you free).

Ahead of time the planning team should create the list by mixing truth statements from the Bible (Proverbs about truth and wisdom and the words of Jesus are easy places to start) with proverbs and quotes about truth and wisdom from cultures around the world (search on the Internet for "proverbs about truth," "proverbs about wisdom," "quotes about truth," or "quotes about wisdom"). You will need 12 to 15 statements total. The list might look something like the following:

1. Jesus said, "I am the way, and the truth, and the life." *(True; John 14:6 NRSV)*

2. "God makes many plans, but a man must follow his heart." *(False; not in the Bible)*

3. "The human mind plans the way, but the LORD directs the steps." *(True, Proverbs 16:9 NRSV)*

Station 3. Independence Day Scavenger Hunt

What You'll Need

Volunteer: station host
Scavenger hunt list
Small prizes for winning teams if desired
   (pinwheels, flags, Red Hots candies, etc.)

Note: This hunt can take place both inside and outside your church, as well as in the neighborhood around your church. Your planning team will need to decide the boundaries. The total hunting time will be about 20 minutes, with 5 minutes before and after for initial directions and verification of winning team items.

The host should welcome participants and ask them to form teams of 4–6 people. Individual families can split up and mix with older adults and singles. Each team should be given a scavenger hunt list. Explain that teams have 20 minutes to find objects inside or outside the church that represent the Independence Day–theme items on the list. The host will be the final judge as to whether the object accurately symbolizes the list item. Remind teams to be gentle with church property and be ready to put items back where they found them when the hunt is over.

The list includes:

1. Something red
2. Something white
3. Something blue
4. Something that makes noise
5. Something with the number 4 on it
6. Something that represents truth
7. Something that represents life
8. Something that represents liberty/freedom
9. Something that represents happiness
10. Something that represents struggle/sin
11. Something that represents summer

Fellowship

Ideally this program will include a picnic or barbecue; however, your planning team will need to decide how you want your event to flow. Do you want to start with a meal, then go to the faith stations, and close with worship? Or do you want to open with worship, go to the faith stations, and end with the picnic or red, white and blue snacks? Each event can be tailored to your group's needs and time constraints. Just be sure to include a time of fellowship in your program, whether a full meal or light refreshments.

Note: An option to add during the fellowship time would be to have a band come and play patriotic music during or after the meal. The planning team may also want to have a few Fourth of July–themed crafts available as part of the picnic entertainment. See this book's website (www.forallgenerations.com) for directions for "'Fire Cracker' Hunt" and "Virtual Fire Crackers" from Elizabeth Crisci's book *Celebrate Good Times* (Judson Press, 2005).

CHAPTER 16

July
Arts Festival

Program Focus: A multimedia celebration of the arts in your church

Key Verse: "Bezalel and Oholiab and every skillful one to whom the LORD has given skill and understanding to know how to do any work in the construction of the sanctuary shall work in accordance with all that the LORD has commanded" (Exodus 36:1 NRSV).

Purpose:
a. To showcase examples of artwork by congregation members
b. To offer hands-on opportunities with art and different media
c. To celebrate art and its role in a faith community

Leader Background

From the first recorded praise song lyrics in Exodus 15 (Miriam's song of praise), the arts have long been a part of our faith traditions. Music, poetry, and stories have formed the foundation of worship since the time of our Bible ancestors. In addition, God's people have given glory and honor to God, as well as have expressed their joys and struggles with faith, through their God-given creativity and talents. Art has been used to celebrate God, understand God, share God, and reveal the nature of God, and this program will acknowledge the importance of the arts in our faith and their role in deepening our connection to our Lord and Savior.

Note: The station rotations are not formally scheduled in this program. They will run on a drop-in basis, so participants can spend as much or as little time in the different stations as they like. In addition to the faith stations, the planning team should invite artists from the congregation, as well as artists from the local community, to come in and either display their art or lead hands-on demonstrations using their media. The team should consider a wide variety of art, including visual (painting, sculpture and pottery, photography, videos, etc.), literary (poems, fictional stories, nonfiction articles, devotionals, prayers, etc.), and performing (instrumentalists, singers, actors/actresses, dancers, storytellers, etc.). While this event can be run on a volunteer basis, the planning team may want to utilize a budget to provide materials for the visiting artists' hands-on activities and/or pay a small stipend to visiting artists. If using all volunteers, be especially dedicated to writing thank-you notes to all participating artists and offer to let them display their business cards/artwork at their stations or list them in your worship bulletin or newsletter or on your church website (possibly with a link back to their websites).

Note: Worship will be a featured portion of this event and is scheduled for the last hour of this program. Upon arrival, participants can choose to go to the faith stations of their choice to be involved in preparing materials for worship (banners, skits, readings, songs, liturgical dances, etc.) and/or they can participate in the demonstrations and hands-on activities provided by your visiting artists.

Your planning team should meet with your church's worship planners to determine the best content and flow for the service, but the goal is to fully celebrate the arts. The choir or praise team may want to prepare special music to share. The drama team may want to provide the main message through a drama rehearsed ahead of time. Have key pieces in place but be able to add in participant-generated contributions the day of the program (see stations below). Keep in mind that you will likely have children of all ages in this service, so it may be preferable to plan for a variety of content pieces instead of following a more traditional order of worship.

Faith Stations

Station 1. Worship Banners

What You'll Need

Volunteer: station host

Sections of felt, burlap, or canvas to serve as the
    banner background (approximately 3' x 5')

Fabric scraps and trim

Fabric markers

Scissors

Craft glue or hot glue

1/2" dowel rods 6" longer than the width of your
    banners (1 per banner)

3' sections of ribbon (1 per banner)

List of key verses/themes for the worship banners
    (per planning team)

Note: Ahead of time the planning team should create a list of key "arts" verses from the Bible and/or a list of themes. (Use a concordance or search on a website like www.biblegateway.com under the keywords of *dance, dancing, song, singing, praise, praising, music, artisan, designer, beauty,* or *create.*) The team may

choose to let participants decide which banners to create or may assign a list of verses/themes to be completed during the rotations. The banners will be carried into worship by the participants.

The host should welcome participants and explain that they will be creating banners that celebrate the arts for use in worship that day. Give instructions according to the planning team's preparations; however, the general plan is that participants will be writing out or symbolizing a key verse using the additional fabric, trim, and fabric markers on a banner background. When the banner is complete, assist in folding over the top edge and applying a line of hot glue to make a pocket for the dowel rod. A length of ribbon can then be tied to either end of the rod next to the edge of the banner to form a hanger. Recruit a volunteer from each banner-making group to carry the banner into worship.

Station 2. Wonderful Words

What You'll Need

Volunteer: station host

Bibles

Concordances

Bible commentaries

Paper

Pens

Bible-time costumes (as needed)

Note: Ahead of time, the planning team should come up with a list of key Scripture passages for the worship team to read or interpret through the arts. Search in a concordance or online at www.biblegateway.com for verses that declare the glory and majesty and creativity of God.

The host should welcome participants and invite them to read through the selected verses and work individually or in a group to do the following:

1. Interpret the passage in a short skit or dramatic reading.

2. Write a short prayer about the theme of the verses or incorporating the verses.

3. Write a short poem about the theme of the verses.

Note: The host may want to cross off the verses as they are chosen so that there is no duplication.

These creations can be incorporated into the worship service as desired by the planning team. The host should keep a list of those who wish to participate.

Station 3. Make a Joyful Noise

What You'll Need

Volunteers: station host, worship leader
Rhythm instruments (tambourines, wood blocks, maracas, etc.)
CDs of familiar praise songs and hymns

The host should welcome participants and invite them to make a joyful noise to the Lord by choosing a song from the CD and accompanying it with rhythm instruments or singing along. If the individual/group wants to share this in worship, encourage them to choose a short song or select one verse. Participants could also choose to create movements to accompany a song and then share this in worship. The host should keep a list of who would like to participate in the worship service and with which song.

Station 4. Art from the Heart

What You'll Need

Volunteers: station host, station assistant
Variety of art supplies (watercolor paints/brushes, watercolor paper, drawing paper, colored pencils, oil pastels, Sculpey clay or assorted colors of Model Magic [especially good for younger children], etc.)
Variety of colors of yarn
Large craft sticks (for God's Eyes)
Tape or sticky-tack
Bibles
Concordances

The host should welcome participants and invite them to create pictures or sculptures that reflect their love for God, their faith in God, the beauty of God's creation, etc. As they finish their creations, the station assistant can hang the pictures or display the sculptures and God's Eyes (see the following directions) in the fellowship area. Participants can take their creations home at the end of the program.

Note: If you prefer to work from an actual pattern, check out a craft book from the library or search "God's eyes" on the Internet.

To begin the God's Eye craft, cross 2 craft sticks at the centers and secure with yarn (can also be glued in addition to being tied with the yarn). The yarn is then wrapped over and around each stick, moving in a circular pattern so that a center forms, about 1" across. Participants should choose a different color yarn for the next circle in the pattern. Start the new color by tying its end to the end of the first yarn and knotting it securely on the back of the eye. Continue wrapping the new color over and around until you have another inch of weaving. Repeat this process with a third color, which will become the outside of "God's eye." When finished, tie it off to the yarn on the back and tape it to the stick to secure it.

Station 5. Additional Art Game Stations

Depending on how the planning team has organized this event, the visiting artists may have additional hands-on art activities for the participants. Your team may want to create a schedule listing the stations and rotation times or indicating whether events are free-flowing until worship time.

In addition, the planning team may want to set up a station with the following art party games taken or adapted from Elizabeth Crisci's *Celebrate Good Times* (Judson Press, 2005):

Draw to Win

Supplies needed: slips of paper, blank drawing paper, markers, small prizes (optional)

In advance, write the name of various objects on small slips of paper. Divide the group into teams of 8–10 to compete against each other in drawing. In this game the host hands a slip of paper with the name of an object to the representative of each team, who races back to the team and begins drawing silently. When one team guesses the object correctly, they change representatives and continue for about 10 drawings. The team that guesses the most pictures correctly wins and members receive a prize.

Curlique

Supplies needed: paper with curly scribble on it, 1 per person (all the same); drawing pencil or dark marker, 1 per person; small candy prizes

Give each person a paper with the same curly scribble on it. Each player creates a drawing that includes the scribble, then names and signs his or her artwork. Allow 5 minutes to draw, and then have each person display his or her creation. Reward every artist with applause and a piece of candy.

Art Foolishness

Supplies needed: piece of drawing paper, 1 per person; sharp pencil, 1 per person; watercolor paints and brushes, colored pencils

Each guest sketches the outline of a picture, and then drawings are passed around so that each person gets someone else's. Everyone colors in the picture he or she received and returns the picture to the original artist.

Note: The art games station will also need a station host to give directions and facilitate the games.

Worship

The planning team should work with the church worship director, as well as this event's main worship leader volunteer, to create an overall order of worship for this event, which will celebrate the arts in a multimedia approach, as well as incorporate the participants' contributions created that day. This service will likely be longer than the typical intergenerational program's worship. Plan your schedule accordingly. Consider concluding with this prayer:

> O God, we thank you for creating each of us, artists, in your image. We ask for the filling of your Holy Spirit, that through our hands and eyes and voices we may experience the wonders of your love. May we proclaim the astounding mystery of creation through the beauty of art in all its forms, and make you known through the spirit of our creativity, which begins and ends in you. Amen.[1]

Fellowship

The bulk of this program will be filled with the faith stations and visiting artists' demonstrations and then worship. Because of the creative nature of this event, it may work best to serve light refreshments in one area at the end of worship so that artwork does not get damaged by messy fingers.

Note

1. Adapted from Sue Ellen Echard, "Gathering Prayer for a Group of Artists," in Brad Berglund, *Reinventing Worship: Prayers, Readings, Special Services, and More* (Valley Forge, PA: Judson Press, 2006), 139.

CHAPTER 17

July
Evening Vacation Bible School: Dr. Seuss and Friends

Leader Background

Summer is a wonderful time to try an intergenerational program if you haven't already. Schedules are more relaxed, the weather is more cooperative, and the days are longer, allowing for more outdoor activities. In addition, while summer vacations may remove some volunteers from the pool, the planning team may be able to find new recruits among college students or school teachers home on break. And churches frequently try alternative programming in the summer to work around seasonal attendance issues, so this may be the perfect time to dip your toes into the intergenerational program pond without anyone knowing your fear of the water!

Sample Schedule

5:50–6:15 Gathering time/Registration

6:15–8:15 Station rotations

8:15–8:45 Worship

8:45–9:00 Fellowship/Snacks

Note: Ahead of time, the planning team should hold a collection drive for canned and boxed food, toiletries and cleaning products, and/or school supplies and backpacks (contact area school districts for their school supply lists and request accordingly). The team should also contact a local moving company to get a donation of small packing boxes. These will be used in Station 3.

Program Focus: Life lessons from Dr. Seuss

Key Verses: "The unfolding of your words gives light; it gives understanding to the simple. . . . Direct my footsteps according to your word; let no sin rule over me" (Psalm 119:130, 133 NIV).

Purpose:
a. To explore making wise choices based on God's Word
b. To explore the spiritual fruit of being kind and generous
c. To come together as a family of faith for study and fellowship

NIGHT 1: ALL YOU NEED IS LOVE

Gathering Time

Volunteer: station host
Sidewalk chalk
Foam or soft rubber ball
Mural paper and markers (if weather does not allow
  for chalk drawing outside)
Assortment of Dr. Seuss books

Begin your evening together with an informal gathering time. If the weather cooperates, allow chalk drawing outside in the parking lot and encourage participants to create Dr. Seuss landscapes with funny trees and wild colors. Have books available for reference or reading. This activity can be done inside on mural paper with markers if the weather does not cooperate. The host can also organize favorite group games like Steal the Bacon (for directions, see p. 85) or a form of ball tag, such as SPUD. Or participants can simply visit with one another until the station rotations begin.

When ready to start rotations, the host should divide the large group into 4 smaller groups, being intentional about blending family groups with singles, older adults, and visitors.

Station 1: Making Wise Choices

What You'll Need

Volunteer: station host/storyteller
The Cat in the Hat by Dr. Seuss (Random House, 1957)
White rectangles of construction paper (approximately
  2" wide by 6" long, 1 per person)
Red rectangles of construction paper (approximately
  2" wide by 1" long, 3 per person)
Black pens/markers
Self-stick address labels preprinted with Psalm
  119:130 and 133 (1 per person)
Glue sticks

The host should welcome participants to the station and invite them to sit in a semicircle. Explain that in this station they will be talking about making wise choices. To help them understand wise and not-so-wise choices, the host should read *The Cat in the Hat*.

After the story, ask participants to break into small groups of 8 and discuss the following questions:

1. Who made the first unwise choice in the story?
2. What happened after the first unwise choice was made?
3. How do you think one unwise choice can lead to another unwise choice?
4. Have you ever made an unwise choice? Tell what happened?
5. How did you get back on the right path and make wise choices again?
6. How do you think God helps you make wise choices?
7. Can you think of one piece of advice from God that tells us how to make wise choices (maybe a Bible memory verse you learned)? Share it with your group.

After the groups have had 10–15 minutes to discuss, ask the groups to share the answers to questions 6 and 7. Then ask the groups to move to the worktables. Each table should have enough red and white rectangles and preprinted Bible verse labels for each person. Each table should also have a supply of black markers and glue sticks.

Explain to participants that they are going to make a Cat in the Hat bookmark to help them remember to make wise choices. Each person should glue 3 red rectangles onto the long white rectangle to make the Cat in the Hat's striped hat. On the red rectangles, each person should write an unwise choice that he or she wants to avoid. On the white rectangles, each person should write examples of wise choices he or she has made or can make. Encourage table groups to talk about their choices before writing them on the bookmark. When participants finish with the choices, they can add a Bible verse sticker to the back side.

Station 2: *How the Grinch Stole Christmas*

What You'll Need

Volunteer: station host
DVD of *How the Grinch Stole Christmas* by Dr. Seuss
  (original 1966 animated classic)
TV/DVD player
Bibles

The host should welcome participants to the station and invite them to gather around the TV/DVD player. Ask the group if anyone has ever seen *How the Grinch Stole Christmas* (most likely yes). Explain that while it's a funny story with silly songs, Dr. Seuss was also trying to give people a message. Ask if any of the children think they know what that message is. Clarify as needed that the story is showing how the Grinch's heart was changed by seeing the Whos still celebrating Christmas and their love for one another. Witnessing that powerful love changed his life. We're going to talk about how God's love can change our lives as Christians.

After initial discussion, play the DVD. When the DVD ends, ask participants to get into groups of 8 and talk about the following questions (give each group a Bible):

1. What was the Grinch's main problem?

2. Have you ever felt like the Grinch, like you didn't get what you deserved or you wanted all the good things for yourself? What happened?

3. What happened to the Grinch's heart? Why?

4. If we're selfish and don't love others the way God loves us, what happens to our hearts?

5. Who has the ability to change our hearts?

6. Read Matthew 22:34-40 in your group. If the Grinch and the Whos of Whoville read these verses, who do you think would understand them better? Why?

After groups have had 10–15 minutes to discuss, close the time in prayer and explain that in the Worship Prep station, participants will have an opportunity to make their hearts bigger by sharing their gifts with others. They will be putting together food or school supply care packages to give to needy families. These packages will be dedicated during the offering time.

Station 3: Worship Prep

What You'll Need

Volunteer: station host, worship leader, drama leader,
  videographer
Video camera, tripod, and tape
Care package supplies (food items, toiletries, cleaning
  supplies, and small packing boxes or school supplies
  and backpacks)
Bibles marked for the story of Samson and Delilah
  (Judges 16:4-31)
Bible-time costumes
Props for Samson and Delilah story (long hair wig,
  ropes, temple pillars, mural paper, markers, etc.)
Songbooks/hymnals or list of familiar songs
Bibles
Concordances
Note cards
Pens

The host should welcome participants, explain the various worship prep options, and invite them to sit at the appropriate worktables. In this station participants will be helping plan the evening's worship service. People may choose to:

- participate in a wise/unwise choices skit featuring Samson and Delilah. Skit preparation will be facilitated by the drama leader who will read through the Samson story with the actors and help them choose roles or prepare props and scenery. The drama leader will help the team practice the skit. When they are ready, the videographer will videotape their performance, which will be shared in worship (all four versions from all four rotations).

- work with the worship leader to write an offertory prayer or a call to worship or choose music for the service. Another option would be for the worship leader to have a few songs chosen and then work with participants to add motions and prepare to be song leaders for the service.

- prepare care packages. The planning team should have handouts with assembly instructions prepared for either the food or school supply care packages. Participants can work to box up the required items and include a "Thinking of You" card with the text of Matthew 22:36-39 written in it.

Station 4: Fellowship Prep

What You'll Need

Volunteers: station host, kitchen crew

Paper plates

Paper cups

Lemonade mix

Pitchers

Veggie pizza supplies (for each pizza you'll need 2 packages of refrigerated crescent rolls, 1 package of light cream cheese, 1 package of dry ranch salad dressing mix, 1 cup of light mayo, and assorted cut up veggies)

Blueberry muffin supplies (muffin mix, eggs, 4 oz. cups of applesauce)

Fresh fruit

Knives

Cutting board

Baking sheets

Muffin tins and paper muffin cups

Nonstick cooking spray

Mixing bowls

Serving bowls

Ahead of time, the planning team and kitchen crew should set up worktables near the kitchen. One or two tables (depending on the total size of your group) can be used for making veggie pizza. One or two tables can be used for making batches of blueberry muffins. One table can be used for cutting up fresh fruit. One work area can be in the kitchen by the sink for the lemonade prep.

The host should welcome participants and explain that they will be helping prepare the snacks for fellowship. Also explain that the planning team has made wise choices in selecting healthy foods to nourish the participants' bodies. Share Proverbs 3:7-8, which talks about wise choices nourishing our bodies.

Participants should first wash their hands with soap. They may then work at any of the prep stations (directions follow). When they are done with food prep, they can help set up tables and chairs and put out paper goods as needed.

Veggie Pizza

2 rolls of refrigerated crescent roll dough

1 package light cream cheese, softened

1 package ranch seasoning

1 cup light mayo

Assorted vegetables (broccoli, carrots, cucumbers, cauliflower, celery, chives, etc.)

Form the crust by spreading out the crescent rolls on a baking sheet sprayed with nonstick cooking spray.

Bake for 10 minutes at 375 degrees. While the crust is baking, mix the cream cheese, mayo, and ranch seasoning. Also chop the veggies into tiny pieces. Allow the crust to cool. Spread with cream cheese mix. Sprinkle veggies on top. Cover with plastic wrap and refrigerate until serving.

Blueberry Muffins

1 box of blueberry muffin mix

1 egg

1 4-oz. cup of applesauce (use in place of oil for fat-free muffins)

Fresh blueberries

In a bowl, mix muffin mix, egg, and applesauce. Add the blueberries from the mix and additional fresh blueberries if desired. Spoon into a muffin tin lined with paper muffin cups. Bake according to package directions.

Fresh Fruit Mini-Skewers

Assorted seasonal fresh fruit

Toothpicks

Serving platters

Cut up fresh fruit into bite-size chunks. Place several chunks of fruit on each toothpick to make mini-fruit skewers. Cover with plastic wrap and refrigerate until serving.

Worship

After the station rotations, gather the entire group in the designated worship area. Make sure that you have a TV/DVD screen and hookup for the video camera to play back the Samson skits. Allow participants to work with the worship leader to lead the service. Open with a few praise songs or hymns. Have a participant read Psalm 119:130, 133 and Proverbs 3:7-8. Play the Samson skits. Dedicate the food packs or filled backpacks to be used for God's glory. Have a leader close in prayer, asking God to help participants make wise choices and use God's Word as a map for their lives.

Fellowship

Following worship, the group can move to the fellowship area and enjoy the healthy snacks that were prepared earlier.

Extension Options

Your planning team may want to extend vacation Bible school beyond a one-night experience. This program lends itself to multiple nights, whether you choose an additional 1 or 4. For full program details, visit www.forallgenerations.com. Program summaries follow below.

NIGHT 2: WE BOW DOWN

Seuss story: *Yertle the Turtle* (Random House, 1958)

Biblical tie-in: Putting others before yourself and valuing all people as children of God as Jesus does with us. Passages include the parable of the rich young ruler and the danger of riches (Mark 10:17-31); the blessing of the little children (Mark 10:13-16) and the Beatitudes (Luke 6:17-26); the parable of the wedding banquet (Luke 14:7-14); and the parable of the great dinner (Luke 14:15-24).

Stations

- Read *Yertle the Turtle* and have small group discussion about people having power over others and using that power for their own betterment.

- Have participants prepare skits (videotaped for worship) on the parable of the rich young ruler (Mark 10:17-31), the blessing of the little children (Mark 10:13-16) and the Beatitudes (Luke 6:17-26), the parable of the wedding banquet (Luke 14:7-14), and the parable of the great dinner (Luke 14:15-24). Each rotation group can work on a different passage to produce four separate skits for worship, or all groups can work on all the passages and choose one to be played during worship.

- Make a turtle banner with symbols of power represented in the sections of the shell.

- Make turtle-shaped cookies.

NIGHT 3: FOR THE BEAUTY OF THE EARTH

Seuss story: *The Lorax* (Random House, 1971)

Biblical tie-in: Being good stewards of God's creation. "God said, 'See, I have given you every plant yielding seed that is upon the face of all the earth, and every tree with seed in its fruit; you shall have them for food. And to every beast of the earth, and to every bird of the air, and to everything that creeps on the earth, everything that has the breath of life, I have given every green plant for food.' And it was so. God saw everything that he had made, and indeed, it was very good. And there was evening and there was morning, the sixth day" (Genesis 1:29-31 NRSV).

Stations

- Read *The Lorax* and have small group discussion about people using and abusing God's creation.

- Neighborhood cleanup. Send rotation groups out into the church property and surrounding neighborhood to clean up garbage. Separate recycling and dispose of properly.

- Church grounds beautification. Trim bushes, pull weeds, plant late summer flowers, etc.

- Worship prep. Choose a psalm to read responsively, act out, or set to music; add motions to creation-theme songs chosen by the worship leader; prepare a liturgical dance; write a creation prayer using each of the letters in the word; create an outdoor worship space with chalk drawings, flower arrangements, seating, etc.

NIGHT 4: IMMORTAL, INVISIBLE GOD ONLY WISE

Seuss story: *Horton Hears a Who* (Random House, 1954)

Biblical tie-in: Christ is the image of the invisible God and through him we become one. "He is the image of the invisible God, the firstborn of all creation; for in him all things in heaven and on earth were created, things visible and invisible, whether thrones or dominions or rulers or powers—all things have been created through him and for him. He himself is before all things, and in him all things hold together" (Colossians 1:15-17 NRSV).

Stations

- Read *Horton Hears a Who* and have small group discussion about people treating others with respect, kindness, and gentleness and working together for a common goal.

- Have a guest speaker from a ministry or mission who serves those without a voice and helps them to help themselves (homeless shelter, prison ministry, foreign missions, etc.).

- Improve listening skills through games that require paying attention and following directions.

- Have a teamwork activity that requires building a sculpture according to specific directions, with each team member having certain abilities and functions in the process.

NIGHT 5: HERE I AM, LORD, SEND ME!

Seuss story: *Oh the Places You'll Go* (Random House, 1990)

Biblical tie-in: Trusting God to guide our lives. "The human mind plans the way, but the LORD directs the steps" (Proverbs 16:9 NRSV).

Stations

- Read *Oh the Places You'll Go* and have small group discussion about trusting God's will and being faithful to God's plans for his people.

- Follow a path of biblical advice. A treasure hunt map contains Scripture verses that can be found in various locations in the church. Only by discovering each clue can the path be completed.

- Make a footprint cross banner by using feet dipped in paint to create a cross on individual banners and a banner for the church. The four points of the cross on the individual banner will also represent places people have "gone" in their lives.

- Make trail mix for the journey and fortune cookies with Bible verses tucked inside.

CHAPTER 18

August
Knit Together: Team Unity

Program Focus: Team building and unity of the Spirit

Key Verses: "But speaking the truth in love, we must grow up in every way into him who is the head, into Christ, from whom the whole body, joined and knit together by every ligament with which it is equipped, as each part is working properly, promotes the body's growth in building itself up in love" (Ephesians 4:15-16 NRSV).

Purpose:
a. To engage participants in team-building activities
b. To explore biblical models of teamwork (e.g., Nehemiah and rebuilding the temple)
c. To celebrate the role of teamwork in kingdom work

Leader Background

Ephesians 4:15-16 says, "But speaking the truth in love, we must grow up in every way into him who is the head, into Christ, from whom the whole body, joined and knit together by every ligament with which it is equipped, as each part is working properly, promotes the body's growth in building itself up in love" (NRSV). Teamwork is hard work at times. Not everyone has the same strengths, talents, and abilities, but God calls us to use our individual strengths, talents, and abilities to serve together as one body—the body of Christ. This program will help participants see the value of teamwork and understand how to practice that spiritual discipline.

Note: In Olympic years, the planning team may want to give the event an overall Olympic theme.

Worship

Opening Song(s): Open your time together with 3–5 songs of praise and worship that support the theme of teamwork and unity. Possibilities include "All People That on Earth Do Dwell," "All Hail the Power of Jesus' Name," "Blest Be the Tie That Binds," "Bind Us Together," "We Are One in the Spirit," "We Are the Body," "Make Us One."

Scripture Reading: Ephesians 4:15-16

Time of Prayer: Invite participants to lift up examples of people working together for the sake of the kingdom. The leader can also pray with an emphasis on unity and teamwork in the name of Jesus Christ.

Closing Song: "They'll Know We Are Christians by Our Love"

Faith Stations

Station 1. Nehemiah the Builder

What You'll Need

Volunteers: station host, station assistant

Plastic swords and spears

100 paper bags (mix of sizes)

Mural paper with a stone wall drawn on it (Wall should be 10'–12' in length and appear in poor condition, broken and unlevel. Holes should be cut in the mural for missing stones. The other stone sizes should match the assorted paper bag sizes that will be taped onto the wall, symbolizing the reconstruction.)

Tape

The host should welcome participants and explain that they will be taking part in the story of Nehemiah, a faithful Jew who led the effort to rebuild the wall around the holy city of Jerusalem. Ask for volunteers and divide them into the burden bearers, the builders, and the defenders. Also find volunteers to serve as Sanballat and Tobiah, who plot against the Jews and try to organize attacks and schemes to get Nehemiah out of the picture. Two adults should hold either end of the wall mural.

The first part of the story involves the rebuilding of the gates and does not use the volunteers. The second part of the story involves the rebuilding of the wall itself. The station assistant will be responsible for cuing the volunteers. At first, all volunteers will carry paper bags (representing wall stones) over to the wall mural and tape them in place, matching them up to the rectangular stone outlines drawn on the wall, as the host begins to read about reconstruction of the wall.

Later as the host starts to describe the opposition to the work, the volunteers should be split up into their groups: burden bearers, builders, and defenders. The defenders should take up a weapon and step behind the mural and peek out of the holes in the wall or above the wall (can stand on a chair). The burden bearers should carry a bag/stone in one hand and a weapon in the other. The builders should be positioned along the wall ready to tape on the stones when the stones are handed to them. The station assistant should also cue Sanballat and Tobiah to shake their heads, frown, point their fingers at the workers, and turn their backs and whisper as if they are plotting and planning to destroy Nehemiah and the wall.

Both the station host and station assistant should be familiar with Nehemiah 1–5, with the host being comfortable enough to tell the story and allow for the volunteers to act out certain parts. After the story, the host can ask participants to break into small groups and answer the following questions:

1. How did Nehemiah show his faithfulness to God?

2. It was Nehemiah's idea to rebuild the wall, but he didn't do it by himself. How did the wall get rebuilt?

3. What do you think the Jews in Jerusalem learned from Nehemiah?

4. Can you think of a time when you needed to work together with a group of people to get something done? Tell your group about it.

5. What kinds of church work (mission work) can be accomplished when God's children work together instead of separately?

Station 2. Building the Walls

What You'll Need

Volunteers: station host

Mini-marshmallows (1 bag per group)

Tubs of white frosting (1 tub per group)

Large heavy-duty paper plates (1 per group)

Plastic knives

Graham crackers (1 plastic pack per group)

Small prizes (medals, ribbons, etc.) for winning team members (optional)

The host should welcome participants and ask them to divide into groups of four. Families can split up and join with older adults and singles to form new teams. Explain that in Bible times cities had walls going all the way around their borders to protect them from enemies. When the walls were damaged, the city was vulnerable to attack. In the Nehemiah story, Nehemiah is called by God to rebuild the wall around the holy city of Jerusalem. In this station, teams will be working to recreate the city of Jerusalem and the wall that surrounded it using teamwork. All group members need to participate equally. The first task is to create on the plate one or more city buildings out of graham crackers and frosting. The second task is to build a wall all the way around the city out of mini-marshmallows. The team that has the most complete city and the most complete wall will win a prize.

Note: The planning team may also want to put a large supply of cardboard or wooden building blocks in this space to entertain participants who finish before other teams.

Station 3. Team Sports

What You'll Need

Volunteers: station host, station assistants to be
    timekeepers and measurers

Masking tape

Permanent markers

Stop watches

Sturdy foam dinner plates or sponge flying disc

Paper

Pens

Sponge ball

Heavy cardboard gift wrap tube wrapped in newspaper
    and packing tape for extra strength and weight

Newsprint or poster board

Simple ribbons/medals for first-, second-, and third-
    place winners in each event and/or a teamwork
    medallion for all participants

Note: This station is best done outside or in a gym or fellowship hall. Ahead of time, the planning team will mark the course with tape for the cross-country race and the 500-inch dash.

The host should welcome participants and ask them to divide into teams of 6–8 people. Family groups can split up and realign with older adults and singles. The teams will be sending representatives to compete in the following events: cross-country race, discus throw, shot put, 500-inch dash, and javelin throw. Each team member should compete in at least one event. The events are as follows:

1. *Cross-Country Race.* This event consists of "race walking" around a route marked with tape throughout different rooms and corridors of the area or on an outdoor course.

2. *Discus Throw.* Participants stand behind a line and throw, discus-style, a round foam dinner plate or a sponge flying disc. Let each contestant have 2 tries. The 3 with the longest throws receive appropriate prizes. If space is limited, instead of going for the longest actual throw, ask contestants to hit a sign with a distance, such as 80 meters, 100 meters, or "Out of the Stadium" indicated on it.

3. *Shot Put.* Contestants gather at a starting line. One at a time they throw a sponge ball shot put–style. Mark the landing spots with the contestant's name on masking tape until all have tried. Give out prizes to the longest distances.

4. *500-Inch Dash.* Measure out 500 inches. Time contestants as they run, one at a time. Winners receive appropriate medals.

5. *Javelin Throw.* Mark a line. Each contestant throws the cardboard tube javelin from behind the line. Have two or more judges mark where the javelin lands with masking tape and the contestant's name. Award appropriate prizes.

In addition to individual medals or ribbons, award teamwork ribbons or medals to all participants.

Note: Sports activities were taken from the "Track and Field Day" party in Elizabeth Crisci's book *Celebrate Good Times* (Judson Press, 2005).

Fellowship

Ideally this program should close with a time of fellowship. Consider serving healthy snacks like popcorn, cut up fruits and vegetables, and water or sports drinks. Or, if serving a full meal, offer a spaghetti dinner, which is what many athletes eat the night before a big race or competition. However, your planning team will need to decide how you want your event to flow. Just be sure to include a time of fellowship in your program, whether it be a full meal or light refreshments.

CHAPTER 19

August
Back to School Celebration

Leader Background

Proverbs 7:1-3 says, "My child, keep my words and store up my commandments with you; keep my commandments and live, keep my teachings as the apple of your eye; bind them on your fingers, write them on the tablet of your heart" (NRSV). Looking to God as the master teacher and Jesus as the model-student-turned-teacher, churches have an opportunity to celebrate both learners and educators, in and out of the church setting.

Faith Stations

Station 1. Jesus the Student, Jesus the Teacher

What You'll Need

Volunteer: station host

Study Bibles

Bible commentaries

Assorted story supplies

Poster board

Paper

Markers

Scissors

Seed packets

2 bags of dirt

Paper cups

Paper plates

Books and Bibles

Handful of rocks

Program Focus: Value of education and educators

Key Verse: "And [Jesus] said, 'Let anyone with ears to hear listen!'" (Mark 4:9 NRSV).

Purpose:

a. To recognize educators (of public and private schools and Sunday school) and their contributions as servants and leaders in community

b. To celebrate students as individuals and as achievers

c. To explore spiritual themes of how we are called to be both lifelong learners and teachers in the community of faith

The host should welcome participants and explain that, in groups, they will be reading and teaching a Bible story in this station. Jesus grew up learning the Old Testament stories by heart. He later taught with stories because they were more personal and helped him teach the truth that God wants to be in relationship with us. Explain that each group will receive a different Bible passage, and members need to decide how to teach this story to the other group. They can interpret the passage as a drama; they can involve the other group in an interactive retelling; they can use props or objects to illustrate the story (take from the story supply box or find their own items around the room or church)—it's completely up to them how to teach the story.

Divide the group in half. If there are more than 10–12 people in a group, divide into multiples of 2 (i.e., 4 groups, 6 groups, 8 groups). Half will teach Luke 2:41-52. The other half will teach Mark 4:1-20. Give the groups 15–20 minutes to work, circulating among the groups and offering assistance as needed. After the prep time, ask the groups to take turns teaching their stories. When the groups are finished, ask everyone to respond to this question: "What, if anything, did you learn from this story when you had to teach it to someone else?" Groups should share their answers with the large group.

Station 2. Apple of Your Eye

What You'll Need

Volunteer: station host
Red, yellow, green, and brown construction paper
Scissors
Pens
Markers
Sheets of self-stick address labels preprinted with the text of Proverbs 3:1; Proverbs 4:2; Proverbs 7:2; and Job 36:22
Bibles
Concordances
Tree drawn on a sheet of mural paper (approximately 6'–8' high)
Red and yellow construction paper apples to go on tree (at least 1 per person)
Craft sticks (2 per person)
Red, blue, green, brown, and white yarn

The host should welcome participants and gather them in a semicircle. Ask the group if they know what it means to be the apple of someone's eye. After getting responses, read from Proverbs 7:1-3. Then ask the group the following questions:

1. Why do you think God wants us to keep his teachings as the apple of our eye?

2. How do you think we can do that?

Ask participants to divide into smaller groups of 4–6 people. Families can split up and realign with singles and older adults. Ask the groups to complete the following tasks:

1. Think of something that you can do because someone taught you how to do it. What is that skill, and who taught you? Don't say it out loud yet. Once everyone has thought of something, go around your group and act out the skill. See if your group can guess. As an added challenge, see if they can guess who taught you that skill.

2. Think of something you learned recently. Who taught you that thing, and what is it? Again, try to have your group guess the thing and the teacher.

3. What makes a good teacher? (What qualities does he or she have to have?)

4. What makes a good student? (What qualities does he or she have to have?)

5. Can a teacher be a student and a student be a teacher? How?

When groups are finished discussing, each person should cut out an apple from construction paper and write his or her name along with the name of his or her favorite teacher. If participants would like to add a Bible verse to the apple, they can do so from the preprinted options, or they can find one that better fits their teacher. When finished, participants can tape their apples to the tree. The names on this apple tree will be lifted up in worship today.

The last activity that participants can do is to make a weaving to remind them that God's teachings are to be the apples of our eyes. This craft follows a God's-eye pattern in which 2 craft sticks are crossed and secured with red yarn (see directions in Chapter 16, page 61). The red yarn is surrounded with green, brown, or blue yarn to represent the person's eye color. White yarn is used to finish the weaving, as the outside eye color.

Station 3. Bible Baseball

What You'll Need

Volunteer: station host

Small apple-theme prizes if desired (erasers or pencils with apple designs, apple-flavor gum or candy, fresh apples, etc.)

Chairs for bases/seats

Bible with concordance (for checking answers as needed)

The host should welcome participants and divide into 2 teams of 8–10 people. Family groups can split up and realign with older adults and singles. The teams will be working together to answer the Bible Baseball questions (taken from Elizabeth Crisci's book *Celebrate Good Times,* Judson Press, 2005). If the group is larger than 20 people, consider having two games going at once and form smaller teams. Depending on the ages and level of participants' Bible knowledge, you may also want to offer the "switch hitter" rule, which allows the "batter" to receive help from teammates before answering. Encourage all team members to participate.

Set up the "diamond" using chairs. As each player comes "up to bat," he or she chooses a difficulty category (single, double, triple, or home run) and the pitcher (a leader who is not on either team) asks the question and calls the answer a "hit" (correct) or an "out" (incorrect). Players advance bases accordingly and switch sides after three outs.

Singles:

1. Who was the first man? *(Adam)*
2. What did God do on the seventh day of Creation? *(rest)*
3. What swallowed Jonah? *(a big fish/whale)*
4. Name one of the Ten Commandments. *(see Exodus 20)*
5. Who built the ark? *(Noah)*
6. Who was the first woman? *(Eve)*
7. What was the secret of Samson's strength? *(his uncut hair)*
8. Who was thrown into a den of lions? *(Daniel)*
9. In how many days did God create the world? *(six)*
10. What happened three days after Jesus died? *(He arose.)*
11. What is the last book of the Bible? *(Revelation)*
12. Who was Jesus' mother? *(Mary)*
13. Where was Jesus born? *(in a stable or in Bethlehem)*
14. What is the first book in the Bible? *(Genesis)*
15. Who baptized Jesus? *(John the Baptist)*

Doubles

1. Who led the slaves out of Egypt? *(Moses)*
2. Who is the oldest man in the Bible? *(Methuselah)*
3. Psalm 23 says, "The Lord is my _____." *(shepherd)*
4. What two parts is the Bible divided into? *(Old and New Testament)*
5. Who had a coat of many colors? *(Joseph)*
6. Name two apostles. *(See Matthew 10:2-4.)*
7. Name all four Gospels. *(Matthew, Mark, Luke, John)*
8. What city's walls tumbled down when Joshua marched around it? *(Jericho)*
9. How many times did Peter deny Jesus? *(three)*
10. How many books are there in the Bible? *(66)*
11. Quote any verse from the Bible.
12. How many days did it rain in the Noah story? *(40)*
13. Who received the Ten Commandments? *(Moses)*
14. What book comes after Psalms? *(Proverbs)*
15. What did John the Baptist eat? *(locusts and wild honey)*

Triples

1. Where did Jesus perform his first miracle? *(Cana or a wedding)*
2. Recite John 3:16 *(Check quote in Bible.)*
3. Who came to Jesus at night? *(Nicodemus)*

4. Name one Old Testament prophet that begins with *I, M,* or *Z.* *(Isaiah, Micah, Malachi, Zephaniah, or Zechariah)*

5. Name a New Testament book that is not one of the Gospels.

6. Name a book of the Bible that is named for a woman. *(Ruth, Esther)*

7. What did Jesus tell us to do to our enemies? *(Love them.)*

8. Who was Moses' brother? *(Aaron)*

9. What is the longest book in the Bible? *(Psalms)*

10. Who was the friend of Shadrach and Meshach? *(Abednego; also Daniel or Belteshazzar)*

11. Who was knocked to the ground by a bright light on his way to arrest the followers of Jesus? *(Saul or Paul)*

12. What is the last book of the Old Testament? *(Malachi)*

13. What was Jesus' first miracle? *(He turned water into wine.)*

14. Who were the first people to visit the baby Jesus? *(shepherds)*

15. Who did Mary visit after she found out she was going to have a baby? *(Elizabeth)*

Home Runs

1. Who was Isaac's father? *(Abraham)*

2. Name a fruit of the Spirit? *(see Galatians 5:22)*

3. What New Testament book tells the story of the early church? *(Acts)*

4. Where was Jesus baptized? *(the Jordan River)*

5. Who did Jesus raise from the dead? *(Lazarus; Jairus's daughter; the widow's son)*

6. Who were the first twins? *(Jacob and Esau)*

7. Where did Moses receive the Ten Commandments? *(Mount Sinai)*

8. Which king built the first temple? *(King Solomon)*

9. Recite one of the Beatitudes. *(Matthew 5:3-10)*

10. Who was king of Israel before David? *(Saul)*

11. Who was Moses' sister? *(Miriam)*

12. Which king saw the handwriting on the wall? *(Belshazzar)*

13. What did Jesus celebrate in Jerusalem at age 12? *(Passover)*

14. Where did Noah's ark land? *(Mount Ararat)*

15. Where did Jesus grow up? *(Nazareth)*

Worship

Opening Song(s): Open your time together with 3–5 songs of praise and worship that support the theme of teaching and learning. Possibilities include "Be Thou My Vision," "O Master, Let Me Walk with Thee," "'Tis the Gift to Be Simple," "Thy Word," "Show Me How to Live," "Teach Me Your Ways."

Scripture Reading: Psalm 119:26-32

Time of Prayer: Using the apple tree created in station 2, the leader can give thanks for each teacher named, as well as ask all teachers—private school, public school, Sunday school—to stand and be recognized. Depending on the group size, the leader may ask them to come forward and for participants to come lay hands on them during prayer.

Closing Song: "The B-I-B-L-E" or "Ancient of Days"

Fellowship

Ideally this program should close with a time of fellowship. Consider serving apple-theme snacks like cut up apples and caramel dip, apple pie, dried apples, etc. If serving a full meal, the planning team may want to set up a buffet with school lunch menu choices or serve peanut butter and jelly or bologna sandwiches and other brown bag options. However, your planning team will need to decide how you want your event to flow. Just be sure to include a time of fellowship in your program, whether a full meal or light refreshments.

CHAPTER 20

September
Labor Day

Leader Background

With the Industrial Revolution came much progress but also much sacrifice on the part of workers. In the late 1880s, the average American worked 12-hour days, seven days a week. Children were also hired out as cheap, expendable labor. By 1882 American labor unions had had enough. On September 5 they gathered 10,000 workers and marched from Union Square to City Hall in New York City in the first-ever Labor Day parade to protest working conditions and demand improvements. Individual states began to pass legislation creating a Labor Day holiday to acknowledge the contributions of American workers to the progress of the nation. However, it was not until 1894 that the U.S. Congress made the first Monday in September a national holiday. In keeping with the original purpose of Labor Day, the holiday is still celebrated with parades and festivals across the United States. Many churches in the United States recognize the Sunday before Labor Day as Labor Sunday.

Worship

Opening Song(s): Open your time together with 3–5 songs of praise and worship that support the theme of work and good works. Possibilities include "God of Grace and God of Glory," "O God of Every Nation," "Let Justice Flow Like Streams," "Precious Lord, Take My Hand," "Give Us Clean Hands," "Fearfully and Wonderfully Made," "From the Inside Out," "God Is Great."

Scripture Reading: Psalm 105:1-6

Time of Prayer: Take this time to lift up all workers who are using their gifts and talents to do good, honest work. Pray for those who are looking for work and wanting to be useful. Pray that all people will continue to do good works, not to be saved but as a grateful response to salvation.

Closing Song: "My God, How Wonderful You Are" or "Let the Redeemed"

Program Focus: Celebration of work and working for God

Key Verse: "All must test their own work; then that work, rather than their neighbor's work, will become a cause for pride" (Galatians 6:4 NRSV).

Purpose:
a. To explore God's definition of work and works
b. To thank those who work in the world to support their families, their church, and their communities
c. To celebrate the resting period that comes after hard work, following God's model

Faith Stations

Station 1. What Is Work?

What You'll Need

Volunteer: station host
Worker's Walk map (see explanation below)
Assorted workers and job props (see explanation below)
Self-stick address labels with Bible verses printed on
 them (1 verse per station)

Ahead of time, the planning team should recruit 5 or 6 volunteers from the congregation who work in a nonministerial job but believe they are using their God-given talents and gifts to work for the glory of God. The workers will be talking to small groups of travelers who are following the Worker's Walk map. (This is a map the planning team creates using your church's program space. A worker's name will be listed in a particular classroom or area on the map. The travelers can visit the workers in any order, as long as they visit each one.) At each stop the travelers will meet the worker, and the worker will share his or her story about how he or she ended up in this particular job, what particular gifts he or she is using in this job, and how working in this job lets him or her serve God and give glory and honor to God. It would be best if the workers (with the help of the planning team if necessary) had some props in their locations so they could demonstrate their jobs and/or let people try their jobs (carpenter, nurse, cook, librarian, teacher, etc.). Each worker should talk to each group for approximately 5 minutes and begin by reading the verse assigned to that point on the map, saying, "Consider what the Bible says about work: [read verse]." After the talk, the worker can give each participant a sticker to put on his or her map. Verses can include Psalm 90:16-17; Proverbs 16:1-3; Romans 12:11; 1 Corinthians 3:9; Galatians 6:4; 1 Thessalonians 4:10b-11; and 2 Thessalonians 3:12-13.

The host should welcome participants and explain that they will be using a map to find different workers who will talk to them about their jobs and how, by working, they are also giving glory and honor to God. Each person should receive a map, as each person will also receive a key verse at each stop. Participants should break into groups of 6–8 and may visit the workers in any order.

Station 2. Good Works

What You'll Need

Volunteer: station host
Flip chart/whiteboard and markers
Bibles
Variety of church-based service projects
 (see explanation below; supplies will vary)

The host should welcome participants and gather them in a semicircle. Ask the group to define "good works" and write ideas on the flip chart/whiteboard. Then break the group into three smaller groups and hand each group an envelope. Inside each envelope should be a Bible verse (Ephesians 2:8-10; Titus 3:3-8; or James 2:14-17) and a church service project. One project option will be to help set up for the Labor Day picnic that follows the station rotations. (Participants should see the kitchen or setup crew for instructions on food prep, table setup, decorations, games setup, etc.) Other project options might be weeding the landscaping beds; planting fall flowers; sweeping, mopping, or vacuuming classroom floors; fixing broken furniture or toys; sanitizing classroom toys, furniture, etc. Ask the groups to read the verse and to say a short prayer offering these good works as grateful responses to Jesus' love. The groups should then go to their area and work on their project for 25–30 minutes.

As a follow-up activity, the planning team may want to coordinate with ministry leaders and provide sign-up sheets for participants who would like to continue to volunteer in the area in which they did good works in this program.

Station 3. Sabbath Rest

What You'll Need

Volunteer: station host

Bible-time costume for host

Flip chart/whiteboard and markers

6'–8' section of mural paper with the heading "For to me, I find rest . . ."

Markers

Old magazines

Glue sticks

Scissors

Construction paper sheets cut into quarters, assorted colors

Self-stick labels (about 2" x 3") preprinted with the following verses: Genesis 2:1-3; Exodus 20:8-11; Mark 6:30-32; Hebrews 4:9-11

Self-stick address labels preprinted with the phrase "My next step in having Sabbath rest is . . ."

The host should welcome participants and invite them to sit in a semicircle. You will be telling two stories from the Bible. The focus of the first story is how God rested on the seventh day after creating the world. Tell the Creation story (Genesis 1), with your key point being that God rested when he was done (Genesis 2:1-3). Follow this up with the Fourth Commandment, which says to honor the Sabbath day and keep it holy (Exodus 20:8-11).

Ask the group what God means by the command to honor the Sabbath and keep it holy. Does it mean "Go to church," or does it mean more than that? Let participants answer but also explain that God is asking us to set aside a full 24 hours to rest—to not do "work," however we individually define work. For students that might mean no studying. For writers that might mean no writing. For stay-at-home moms that might mean no cleaning and no laundry. For businesspeople that might mean not answering work e-mails. Depending on a person's work schedule, the day he or she sets aside for Sabbath rest might be different too. Sabbath rest should provide time for bodies to physically rest and spiritually renew. It's not just about no work; it's also about enjoying God's creation. Make a list of ways the group honors the Sabbath on the flip chart/whiteboard.

After discussion invite participants to add to the rest collage. Participants can look through the magazines and cut out pictures of places that symbolize rest to them—a park, the beach, a mountain scene, a cozy cottage, a family spending time together, etc. They can glue these pictures on the mural paper and/or they can draw their own picture on the mural paper.

After contributing to the rest collage, participants can make a "next step" reminder about Sabbath rest by choosing one of the preprinted Bible verses about rest and placing that on a piece of construction paper along with the "My next step . . ." sticker. They can draw or find another picture of a place or scene that symbolizes Sabbath rest to them and place that on the paper along with the stickers (use both front and back sides if necessary). Then they should fill in the "next step" sticker. Families may choose to do one reminder for the whole family. Encourage participants to share their next steps with the people sitting around them.

Fellowship

Ideally this program closes with a traditional Labor Day picnic. The kitchen and setup crews will have had help preparing food and setting up tables/chairs/games through the use of the "Good Works" station participants, so everything should be ready to go when the station time ends. However, the planning team will need to decide how they want the event to flow. Do you want to start with a meal, followed by the faith stations, followed by closing worship? Or, do you want to open with worship, do the faith stations, and end with the picnic? Each event can be tailored to your group's needs and time constraints. Just be sure to include a time of fellowship in your program, whether a full meal or light refreshments.

CHAPTER 21

September
Grandparents Day

Program Focus: Celebrating and honoring grandparents and older adults within the church and without

Key Verses: "The righteous will flourish like a palm tree, they will grow like a cedar of Lebanon; planted in the house of the LORD, they will flourish in the courts of our God. They will still bear fruit in old age, they will stay fresh and green, proclaiming, 'The LORD is upright; he is my Rock, and there is no wickedness in him'" (Psalm 92:12-15 NIV).

Purpose:
a. To find examples of older adults in the Bible who faithfully served God
b. To share examples of wisdom/knowledge possessed by older adults and grandparents
c. To celebrate and honor all grandparents and older adults

Leader Background

West Virginia resident Marian Lucille Herndon McQuade was a grandmother 43 times over; however, she didn't create Grandparents Day because she wanted a little recognition. Mrs. McQuade was a tireless advocate for older adults, having served as the vice chair of the West Virginia Committee on Aging and as a delegate for the White House Committee on Aging. She understood the value of intergenerational connections and worked to get Grandparents Day named an official U.S. holiday. In 1979 President Jimmy Carter declared the Sunday after Labor Day as Grandparents Day. Mrs. McQuade died in 2008, but her legacy continues through the celebration of the holiday. More information on Grandparents Day can be found online at http://www.tcpnow.com/guides/gpdhistory.html.

Note: In publicizing this event, ask participants to invite grandparents or older adult relatives or neighbors to attend this program with them. The station hosts should also make an effort to pair older adults without extended family with family groups that attend. In addition, if using the baby picture fellowship option (see note under Fellowship), make sure to publicize the need for participants each to bring a baby picture to the event.

Worship

Opening Song(s): Open your time together with 3–5 songs of praise and worship that support the theme of wisdom, heritage, and relationships with grandparents and older adults. Possibilities include "Rock of Ages," "May the Circle Be Unbroken," "God of Our Life, through All Our Circling Years," "Love the Lord Your God," "As for Me and My House," "Ancient of Days."

Scripture Reading: Psalm 105:1-6

Time of Prayer: Take this time to lift up all older adults and thank them for their contributions to their families, church, communities, and world. Pray for continued strength and health that God would equip and encourage them to serve all of their days, regardless of age.

Closing Song: "My God, How Wonderful You Are" or "Let the Redeemed"

Faith Stations

Station 1. Our Biblical Grandparents

What You'll Need

Volunteers: station host, 3 storytellers
Bible-time costumes

Ahead of time, the planning team should recruit three older adults to tell the stories of Noah and Zechariah and Elizabeth. The storytellers should dress in costume and tell the stories in first person. The storytellers will need to be very familiar with their texts:

• Noah, Genesis 6–9

• Elizabeth and Zechariah, Luke 1:5-45, 57-80

Ideally the host can split the group in half and send part of the group to visit one storyteller in an adjoining room while the other half stays put. After 15 minutes the host should switch the groups.

After each storyteller finishes his or her story, the storyteller can ask the group the following questions:

Noah

1. How did Noah's age make him the best candidate for the ark-building job?

2. How do you think Noah's sons felt about their 600-year-old father being responsible for building the ark and collecting the animals?

3. If you were Noah's sons, how would you have felt?

4. What do you admire about Noah?

Zechariah

1. What did Zechariah say that got him into trouble?

2. Have you ever been in a situation like Zechariah where you didn't believe something was possible? What happened?

3. What do you admire about Zechariah?

Elizabeth

1. Why do you think God sent Mary to Elizabeth instead of keeping her at home with her mother or near her friends? What did Elizabeth provide or offer to Mary?

2. What do you admire about Elizabeth?

Station 2. Everything Old Is New Again

What You'll Need

Volunteers: station host, older adult volunteers
Antique toys, tools, cooking gadgets, household items, clothing, etc.
Modern counterpart for each antique item
Supplies for baking powder biscuits (flour, baking powder, butter, milk, mixing bowls, biscuit cutters, baking trays, nonstick baking spray, copies of recipe [see page 81])
Store-bought baking powder biscuits (sold in a tube in the refrigerated aisle)
Homemade and store-bought jam (optional)
2 colors of small paper plates
Napkins

Note: This station will need to take place in or near the kitchen. Workstations should be set up with all baking powder biscuit supplies. After groups make the homemade biscuits, the kitchen crew should also bake the store-bought biscuits for comparison.

The host should welcome participants and explain that this station is called "Everything Old Is New Again." Participants will be making old-fashioned baking powder biscuits from scratch and then will taste test them against store-bought biscuits and vote for their favorites. While the biscuits are baking, participants will play a guessing game with old and new products with similar functions.

First, ask participants to divide into groups of 6 or so and ask them to move to the workstations and follow the recipes on the cards. When the biscuits are ready to bake, participants can clean up their areas, wash up, and move to the old-new area.

Ahead of time, the planning team should have recruited volunteers to bring in antique items to display or demonstrate (or let participants try if antiques are not too fragile). The team should also have provided a matching modern item and laid it out on another table (e.g., antique phone/cell phone, early 1900s women's swimsuit/2000+ women's swimsuit, antique tin toy car/remote control car, antique wire whisk or egg beater/cordless mixer, etc.). Let the older adult volunteers explain or demonstrate their antique items one at a time.

After each demonstration, the host should select a volunteer to find the matching modern counterpart on the other table and demonstrate how it works. An alternative to this would be to have a participant, with volunteer supervision, attempt to demonstrate/explain the antique item before choosing the matching modern counterpart.

Continue demonstrations until biscuits are ready. Set store-bought biscuits out on one-color paper plates. Set homemade biscuits out on the other color plates. In addition, you can serve homemade and store-bought jam with the biscuits. Have a tally sheet on the wall where participants can vote for their favorite biscuits according to plate color.

Baking Powder Biscuit Recipe

1 cup flour
2 teaspoons baking powder
1/2 teaspoon salt
3 tablespoons butter plus 1 additional teaspoon
1/2 cup milk
Preheat oven to 425 degrees.

In a mixing bowl, add dry ingredients and mix well. Using a fork, cut 3 tablespoons of butter into the dry mix so that the texture becomes like peas. Add the milk slowly, folding it into the dry mix.

Sprinkle flour on a clean work surface or large cutting board. Gather the dough out of the bowl and pat it onto the work surface. Knead (fold and press) once or twice and flatten to a 1/2" thickness. Cut into 6 pieces with biscuit cutter or knife. Spray a baking tray with nonstick cooking spray and lay pieces on it so that the edges touch. Cut the remaining teaspoon of butter into 6 pieces and place 1 piece on top of each biscuit. Bake at 425 degrees for 12 minutes or until golden brown. Serve immediately.

Station 3. Stories around the Campfire

What You'll Need

Volunteer: station host
S'mores supplies (graham crackers, chocolate bars, big marshmallows, marshmallow roasting sticks, fire pit with fire-making supplies)

Note: This station needs to take place outside around a campfire.

Ahead of time, the planning team should have recruited a team of older adults who like to talk about the "good old days" and who are comfortable talking in groups. This team of storytellers should be divided up so that each rotation group has one or two storytellers to get things started. The host should welcome participants, invite them to sit around the campfire, and introduce the storytellers. While the storytellers tell their stories (these should be personal stories from their childhood and ideally involve some sort of lesson or truth learned from the experience), participants can also roast marshmallows and make s'mores. If time allows, other participants can share stories too.

Fellowship

Ideally this program should close with a time of fellowship with the planning team keeping the fire pit burning and offering other campfire snacks like hot dogs or hot cocoa or apple cider, in addition to extending the supply of s'mores. However, your planning team will need to decide how you want your event to flow. Just be sure to include a time of fellowship in your program, whether a full meal or light refreshments.

Note: A fun fellowship option might be to ask all participants to bring a baby picture of themselves. These could be numbered and displayed on a board or table at the beginning of the event during the gathering time. Each person posting a picture should also print his or her name on a blank sheet of paper. Once all photos are posted, the planning team can copy the list and hand it out to participants. The participants then have to try to match the photo/number with the names on the list. During your closing fellowship time, hold up each picture and announce the name. Award small prizes to the person with the most correct answers if desired.

September | Hispanic Heritage Month (September 15–October 15)

Hispanic Heritage Month was signed into law under President Ronald Reagan in 1988 and celebrates the histories, cultures, and contributions of United States residents whose ancestors came from Spain, Mexico, Central and South America, and the Caribbean. Consider the following possibilities for highlighting Hispanic culture in your church and community.

• **Alza la bandera.** Celebrate the many nations that participate in Hispanic culture by designing a program around the flags of those nations. This makes for a great intergenerational craft, and you can include basic geographical and historical facts related to each nation and its *bandera.* Consider having a flag procession during worship while singing a hymn or praise song in Spanish. Or combine a parade of flags with an arts or food festival.

• **Hablo español.** Design three stations that allow participants of all ages to learn Spanish. At the first, you might provide Spanish translations of familiar Scripture verses; at the second, teach a hymn or praise song in Spanish; at the third, introduce some basic conversational Spanish—phrases such as "My name is ____" or "I love Jesus" or "I speak very little Spanish!"

• **El sabor de nuestra cultura Hispana.** Offer a cooking class each week between September 15 and October 15, featuring child-friendly recipes from Latino nations. Highlight Mexican food one week, Puerto Rican recipes the next week, Cuban cuisine the following week, and so on. Finish off the month with a potluck fellowship for the larger congregation. If you charge a nominal fee, donate the proceeds to a ministry related to teaching ESL or advocacy for immigrant children.

For a wide variety of other ideas that can be converted to station content, visit the following websites:

• www2.scholastic.com/browse/article.jsp?id=3750084
• www.history.com/classroom/hhm/fiesta.html
• www.homeschoollearning.com/units/unit_09-13-01.shtml
• www.smithsonianeducation.org/educators/resource_library/hispanic_resources.html

CHAPTER 22

September
Homecoming Rally

Program Focus: Welcome to our church

Key Verses: "Conduct yourselves wisely toward outsiders, making the most of the time. Let your speech always be gracious, seasoned with salt, so that you may know how you ought to answer everyone" (Colossians 4:5-6 NRSV).

Purpose:
a. To identify ways that your church is welcoming and active
b. To explore how welcoming people to your church welcomes them into relationship with Jesus
c. To create a personal "next step" to invite a friend to come to church or create a program to welcome visitors/newcomers

Leader Background

In the world of high school and college sports, the annual homecoming game is a much-anticipated event each fall. Schools welcome back alumni and encourage the present student body to cheer on their team with a rousing display of school spirit. Should churches be any different?

September is the perfect time for congregations to foster "team spirit," welcoming back members who have been traveling all summer and opening their doors wide to visitors who may be thinking about coming to church for the first time. Holding a homecoming rally gives a church the opportunity to celebrate its identity while extending the hand of Christian friendship into the community.

For more thoughts on welcoming visitors into your church, visit this book's website (www.forallgenerations.com) and read "A View from the Pew" from Malcolm Shotwell's *Creative Programs for Churches* (Judson Press, 1985).

Note: In publicizing this event, ask participants to invite relatives, friends, coworkers, and neighbors to attend this program with them. The station hosts should then make an effort to pair visitors (especially singles or couples) with larger family groups that attend.

The planning team may also wish to run this event as a "block party" with a focus on outdoor games and activities, and send personal invitations to all those residents on the block or in the surrounding neighborhoods.

Worship

Opening Song(s): Open your time together with 3–5 songs of praise and worship that support the theme of church fellowship and always making room for one more. Possibilities include "Joyful, Joyful We Adore Thee," "Lord of Our Life," "We Walk by Faith and Not by Sight," "Walk by Faith," "Shout to the Lord," "Come Home Running."

Scripture Reading: Romans 15:1-7

Time of Prayer: Take this time to pray for the local church and the Christian church in the world, for all believers, and for all of those who are struggling to believe. Pray for visitors who are joining you for the first time and for those who will come. Pray for the spirit of hospitality to be in your church and demonstrated to all who walk through its doors.

Closing Song: "What a Friend We Have in Jesus" or "Step by Step"

Faith Stations

Station 1. Who Are We?

What You'll Need

Volunteers: station host, hunt assistants (see below)
Scavenger hunt list (see right), prizes if desired (preferably a giveaway with the church name, contact information, and logo on it)

Ahead of tim, the planning team should create a scavenger hunt list of items that will provide information about the church's history and identity (past and present). These items should be able to be found in and around the church building or by talking to some key leaders (pastors, other staff, leadership team members, longtime members, etc.). These key leaders (hunt assistants) can be scattered around the church and available to participants during the rotation periods.

The host should welcome participants to the station and ask them to divide into teams of 5–6 people. Family groups can split up and join with friends and visitors or older adults and singles. Facilitate the mixing of old and new faces to maximize the opportunities for new friendships. Distribute the hunt list and tell groups they have 20 minutes to find as many items as possible. Groups should return to the station when finished. Review all teams' findings and award prizes if desired.

Hunt items might include:

1. The date on the church cornerstone
2. The names of the last three senior pastors
3. The total number of classrooms
4. The text of the church mission statement
5. The name of three active ministry volunteers and their areas of service
6. The location of the baptismal font
7. The number of stoves in the church kitchen
8. The brand of coffee served during church fellowship time
9. The sermon title from the previous week
10. The brand name of the main piano, organ, or keyboard
11. The color of the choir robes
12. The color of the drum set
13. Titles of two favorite hymns or praise songs known by the congregation (bonus points if the group can sing the first two lines of the song)
14. The church phone number and/or website address
15. The names of three church programs or ministries geared for kids
16. The names of three church programs or ministries geared for adults
17. The name of one of the oldest church members
18. The name of one of the youngest church members
19. The name of someone who was married in the church
20. The name of someone who was baptized in the church

Station 2. Games Galore

What You'll Need

Volunteer: station host

Easy jigsaw puzzles (10–15 pieces each)

Prizes if desired (preferably a giveaway with the church name, contact information, and logo on it and different from the giveaways used in Station 1)

The station host should welcome participants and explain that part of being involved in a faith community is sharing life with other believers. God calls us to share our concerns, our struggles, and our work (Galatians 6:2). We also share laughter and joy (Romans 12:12, 15), which translates to some good old-fashioned fun with other Christians! Have an assortment of games ready and assemble balanced teams to encourage friendly competition. Play each game for approximately 10 minutes. Feel free to choose other board games or mixers that your congregation knows and enjoys.

Upset the Fruit Basket

In Upset the Fruit Basket, the host assigns a fruit name to each person (use three different names). One person is "It" and stands in the middle of the circle. Remove "It"'s chair before starting play. "It" calls one fruit. All people assigned to that fruit stand up and switch chairs. "It" tries to find a new seat. Whoever is left without a seat becomes the new "It." "It" can also call "Upset the fruit basket," which means that everyone has to get up and find a new seat at the same time.

Puzzle Piece Match-up

In this game the host gives each person a puzzle piece from a collection of children's puzzles. Participants have to find their matching "pieces" and assemble their puzzle. The first team to complete a puzzle wins a prize.

Steal the Bacon

The host divides the group in half, and the two teams line up width-wise at opposite ends of the room. The host then numbers the players in order on each side so that each team has a 1, a 2, a 3, and so on lined up side by side and opposite the person on the other team who has the same number. A center line is marked with tape, and a rag or small, soft object (the bacon) is placed in the middle. When the host calls out a number, those numbered players on each team must race out to the middle and try to "steal the bacon" and make it back to their team without getting tagged. If the player successfully steals the bacon, his or her team gets a point. If the other player tags the thief, the opposite team scores a point.

Station 3. Welcoming Ways

What You'll Need

Volunteer: station host

Bible-time costume

Art supplies (poster board, blank paper, markers, pens, etc.)

The host should welcome participants and invite them to sit in a semicircle. Read Hebrews 13:1-3 and ask the group to respond to this question: "What do these words teach us about being welcoming and kind to strangers?"

After initial discussion, tell the story of Abraham entertaining heavenly visitors. You will need to be very familiar with the text from Genesis 18:1-8. After the story, ask the group these questions:

1. If the Lord visited this church, what kind of welcome would he receive?

2. What if church members didn't know it was the Lord? How are visitors welcomed now?

3. How does this church go outside its doors to invite people to come to church?

After discussion, invite people to move to tables where art supplies are set up. Explain that participants will be creating some kind of welcome message either to invite people to come to church or to welcome them once they arrive. This could take the form of a church cheer, place an ad in the local newspaper, a jingle to sing on the radio, a short public service announcement, a poster to put in store windows, or a poster to hang up in the church. Participants may work individually or in teams. Encourage current members in family groups to split up and join forces with visitors, older adults, and singles to maximize friendship opportunities. Allow about 15 minutes to work. Then display or perform all messages.

Fellowship

Ideally this program closes with a time of fellowship, which may be extended if your planning team chooses the block party theme; however, your team will need to decide how you want your event to flow. If simply serving snacks, consider asking a core group of people to each bring a food item that they would give to a new neighbor . . . like a plate of cookies or homemade banana bread or a favorite pie or cake. However, whether you choose a picnic-style meal or light refreshments, be sure to include a time of pure fellowship in your event.

CHAPTER 23

October
Breads of the World Celebration

Program Focus: International Christian fellowship

Key Verses: "Make every effort to keep the unity of the Spirit through the bond of peace. There is one body and one Spirit—just as you were called to one hope when you were called—one Lord, one faith, one baptism; one God and Father of all, who is over all and through all and in all" (Ephesians 4:3-6 NIV).

Purpose:
a. To identify with Christians across the globe and learn about their struggles
b. To pray for missionaries and believers in other countries
c. To appreciate and celebrate other cultures

Leader Background

In 1936 the Presbyterian Church (USA) started World Communion Day as a way to connect believers across the world through the unifying sacrament of communion. The planners intended for the model to be shared, and by 1940 the Department of Evangelism of the Federal Council of Churches (later National Council of Churches) was encouraging other churches to take part. Almost 75 years later, World Communion Day is still celebrated on the first Sunday in October, connecting brothers and sisters in Christ, not only in the United States, but around the globe, through the sharing of the bread and the cup. Many denominations have their own resources for World Communion Day, so please contact your national office for supplemental resources. Or visit the National Council of Churches USA online at http://www.ncccusa.org/unity/worldcommunionsunday.html.

Note: Ahead of time, the planning team will need to invite a handful of "international" guests to attend this program. The guest list could include members of your own church who have served in the international mission field, short- or long-term. Or the planning team could contact your denomination for missionaries who may currently be visiting or living in your area. Another option is to reach out to area seminaries or Christian colleges, which may have international students (who will be returning to serve in their home countries) who may be willing to come interact with your congregation. Or perhaps you live near churches that have a strong immigrant base in their congregations. Some of these brothers and sisters in Christ may be willing to come share stories of growing up Christian in a foreign country. The underlying goal of this program is to foster unity through diversity.

Worship

Opening Song(s): Open your time together with 3–5 songs of praise and worship that support the theme of international Christian fellowship. Possibilities include "In Christ There Is No East or West," "It Is Well with My Soul," "We Shall Overcome," "Let the Peace of God Reign," "We Speak to Nations," "Hope of Nations." Or use songs representative of the cultures of your invited guests' home countries or mission fields.

Scripture Reading: Ephesians 4:1-7 (read in English and in the native language of one or more of your invited guests)

Time of Prayer: Take this time to pray for the local church and the Christian church in the world, for all believers, and for missionaries who are working to share their faith with others across the globe. If you have international guests and/or missionaries with you, lift them up by name and give thanks for their sharing Jesus with the world.

Communion: Sharing communion together according to your church's beliefs and traditions is an option for this worship service.

Closing Song: "He Reigns" or a song from one of your invited guests' home countries/mission fields

Faith Stations

Station 1. Invited Guests

What You'll Need

Volunteers: station host, international guests
Bible-time costumes
Flip chart/whiteboard and markers

The station host should welcome participants and invite them to gather in a semicircle. If special guests are in this rotation group, introduce them by name and home country or mission field. Tell the story of Paul and his missionary brothers visiting the island of Malta, which led to his two years of teaching in Rome. You will need to be very familiar with Acts 28 in order to tell this story.

After the story, ask participants to divide into groups and answer the following questions:

1. How do you respond when visitors arrive at your home?

2. What do you do to make visitors feel welcome in your home?

3. What did the islanders do when Paul first arrived on Malta?

4. How did the people of Malta continue to make Paul feel welcome and encouraged as he continued his ministry on Malta?

5. Even when Paul was a stranger in a strange land, when he arrived in Rome he rented a house and for two years welcomed guests in to learn about Jesus. What is Paul teaching us about sharing our faith with brothers and sisters around the world?

After groups have had 5–10 minutes to answer the questions, invite one or more of the international guests to share a story from his or her time of living and/or serving God in a foreign country. Dinner will allow for more uninterrupted time to hear stories from all the invited guests.

Note: If possible, ahead of time recruit one of your guests to tell the Acts story or to tell it in his or her native language before or after the English retelling.

Station 2. Culture Connection

What You'll Need

Volunteer: station host
Ethnic games from invited guests' home countries or mission fields
Children's Bibles
Folktale storybooks from invited guests' home countries or mission fields
Music from invited guests' home countries or mission fields

Note: Supplies will vary depending on the nationalities and mission fields of invited guests.

The station host should welcome participants and introduce the invited guests. Explain that as Christians we are part of the family of God, and the family of God does not only include brothers and sisters here in the United States but also around the world. This station includes games, stories, and music from the home countries or mission fields of the invited guests. Participants can move around the station and read folktales, play games, listen to music, or learn a dance from the invited guests' home countries.

Note: If possible, ahead of time recruit several of your guests to help share their culture by asking them to read Bible stories from a children's Bible in their native/mission field language or read folktales from their home country or mission field or teach a game, song, or dance from their country.

Station 3. Breads of the World

What You'll Need

Volunteer: station host
Recipes and ingredients for breads that represent invited guests' home countries or mission fields

Note: These recipes will obviously vary depending on your guest list. Ahead of time, the planning team should collect a bread name and/or recipe from each invited special guest. Recipes can be found online, too, if necessary. From this collection, choose recipes like simple quick or flat breads that will be easy for participants to make and will not require lengthy rise times. (Recipes that won't be made by the participants could be made ahead of time by the guest(s) or planning team and served with the meal.) This station will need to be in the kitchen or in a work area set up outside the kitchen.

The host should welcome participants and invite them to gather in groups of 5–6 around the work areas. Family groups can split up, and the host should facilitate pairing families with older or single adults and invited guests so that fellowship opportunities are maximized. Each group will need a copy of one of the recipes, mixing bowls, spoons, baking pans, and access to the ingredients. Groups should prepare their recipe and then clean up their work area for the next group when finished. Offer help as needed. The kitchen crew will monitor the baking and take the bread out of the oven. The bread can be served during Fellowship.

Fellowship

Ideally this program closes with a time of fellowship over a full meal, which may offer the most relaxed setting for participants to get to know the invited guests better; however, your team will need to decide how you want your event to flow. If doing a full meal, the planning team should facilitate seating one or more invited guests at each dinner table so that participants have a chance to hear their stories of living and/or serving abroad. Another option for dinner would be to serve an ethnic potluck where each participant brings a dish from his or her ethnic heritage. Small signs could be placed by each dish with its name, country of origin, and chefs' names. Be sure to ask one or more of your invited guests to offer grace in his or her native language.

October | Pastoral Appreciation Month

• **Handy Helpers.** Assemble a crew of volunteers of all ages to do household projects for your pastor one weekend. From yard work to painting to organizing closets to making home repairs, show your pastor you value his or her time by giving back the gift of your own time.

• **Care Packages.** Ask congregation members to contribute to a care package for your pastor. A planning team can create a master list. Individuals and/or families could sign up to donate one small item—a selection of tea bags or hot cocoa mixes, hard candies, mints, gum, small packages of tissues, travel-size containers of headache or upset stomach medicine, nail clippers, travel-size spot remover for clothing, bottled water, small denomination gift cards for local coffee shops, restaurants, bookstores, etc.

CHAPTER 24

October
Bright Night Festival

Leader Background

Halloween, like many other holidays, has its roots in both pagan and Christian traditions, dating back 2,000 years to the annual Celtic legends in which the ghosts of the dead caused mischief on the eve of the Celtic new year, October 31. This date also marked the change in seasons, signaling the end of bountiful, vibrant summer and the beginning of dark, lifeless winter. However, in 837 Pope Gregory IV designated November 1 as All Saints Day (Alholowmesse in Middle English, also All-Hallows or All-Hallowmas). Historians believe that the pope was trying to replace a pagan festival in honor of the dead with a Christian one, as Christianity had continued to spread throughout Europe. October 31 eventually became All-Hallows Eve or Halloween, and November 2 became All Souls Day.

Although Halloween spread to the United States, it did so slowly, as early colonists held strict religious views that did not include mystical celebrations. As more and more English and Irish immigrants arrived on the East Coast, however, their imported Halloween traditions of dressing in costume and going from house to house asking for coins or small treats became more commonplace. By the end of the nineteenth century, Halloween was a community-centered, secular holiday with festive costume parties for children and adults as the featured entertainment. Very little of this holiday's religious roots remained, and by the 1950s, Halloween had become a strictly secular holiday geared primarily for children. This program is designed to offer an alternative to traditional Halloween festivities by borrowing a few of the holiday's thematic elements while keeping a faith-based focus.

Program Focus: Becoming lights that shine in the darkness for God

Key Verses: "For once you were darkness, but now in the Lord you are light. Live as children of the light—for the fruit of the light is found in all that is good and right and true" (Ephesians 5:8-9 NRSV).

Purpose:

a. To celebrate Christian community and creativity

b. To provide a faith-focused fall celebration

c. To make a personal "next step" to shine brightly in this world for God

Worship

Opening Song(s): Open your time together with 3–5 songs of praise and worship that support the theme of being lights for Christ. Possibilities include "We Are Marching in the Light of God," "O Radiant Light," "I Am the Light of the World," "This Little Light of Mine," "Oil in My Lamp," "Take My Life."

Scripture Reading: Ephesians 5:8-15

Time of Prayer: Ask participants to share joys and concerns. The leader can pray with special focus on those who are working to be lights for Christ in the world.

Closing Song: "Shine, Jesus, Shine"

Faith Stations

Station 1. The Pumpkin Parable

What You'll Need

Volunteer: station host

Farmer costume (overalls or jeans and work shirt, bandanna, straw hat or John Deere cap, etc.)

The Pumpkin Parable by Liz Curtis Higgs (available online)

Poster board with Earth drawn on it

Small to medium basket

Small yellow construction paper rectangles (approximately 1" x 3", 1 per person)

Pens or markers

Self-stick address labels preprinted with "You are the light of the world" (Matthew 5:14 NRSV)

Tape or glue sticks

Glow necklaces (1 per person, optional)

The station host (dressed as a farmer) should welcome participants and invite them to gather in a semicircle. Ask participants this question before the story: "What do you think it means to be a light for God?"

Then read the story. Afterward ask participants to divide into groups and answer the following questions:

1. What did the farmer have to do to get the pumpkin to grow big and healthy?

2. What do children need to grow big and healthy?

3. What do all people need to do to grow healthy hearts for God?

4. How did the farmer use his big and healthy pumpkin for the glory of God?

5. How can you become a jack-o-lantern and let your faith shine out in the world for God?

After groups have 5–10 minutes to answer the questions, ask groups to think about the following question. Each participant should come up with an answer and then share that answer with their small groups. "What is one 'next step' you can take to shine brightly for God in this world?"

Ahead of time, the host should set up a bushel basket on a table and hide the yellow construction paper strips under it. Next to the basket, set out the preprinted verses and the markers. Tell participants that after they decide on their "next step," they can take a "light" from under the bushel basket, place the verse label on it, and then write down their "next step" and their name. When finished, each person can tape or glue their "light" to the world poster (ideally the "world" will be covered with "light" after all participants have come through the station). As participants leave the station, hand each one a glow necklace if using this option.

Station 2. Pumpkin Decorating Contest

What You'll Need

Volunteer: station host

1 small pumpkin per team

Hot glue gun and glue sticks

Craft glue

Toothpicks

Assorted fabric scraps

Yarn

Glitter glue

Craft paint and brushes

Permanent markers

Pipe cleaners

Construction paper

Scissors

Assorted craft trim and decorations

Old newspapers to cover tables

Bibles

Concordances

Index cards

Pens

Prizes (optional)

The station host should welcome participants and direct them to the worktables covered in newspaper. Ask participants to get into teams of 3–4 people. Family groups can split up and mix with older adults and singles, and the host should facilitate this process. Explain that teams will be competing in a pumpkin decorating contest. The theme is Bible characters, and each team has to make their pumpkin look like a particular character or object from the Bible, plus they have to find a Bible verse that describes or mentions the character or object. Examples include the big fish from the Jonah story, a lion from the account of Daniel in the lions' den, an angel, John the Baptist, baby Moses in a basket, etc. Concordances will help the teams find the verse if they don't know it from memory.

After teams decorate their pumpkins, they should write the character or object name along with the Bible verse on an index card. After all station rotations are complete, transport the pumpkins and cards to the fellowship area. During fellowship time, pumpkins can either be displayed or displayed and voted on for various awards (Most Creative, Most Authentic, Best Use of Yarn, etc.). The planning team can provide certificates to all participants and/or give out special prizes to the top vote-getters.

Station 3. Bright Night Lights

What You'll Need

Volunteer: station host

Glass ivy bowls or recycled glass jars (1 per participant)

Bowls filled with 1" tissue paper squares in orange, yellow, peach, and red

Small votive candles

Bowls of liquid glue thinned with water

Small paint brushes (foam or bristle)

Ahead of time, set worktables with bowls of glue, bowls of tissue squares, brushes, and ivy bowls or jars. The host should welcome participants and direct them to the worktables. Explain that each participant

will be making a glass pumpkin light by brushing the ivy bowl with glue (start with a 2" section) and overlapping squares of tissue paper on the glue. Keep moving around the bowl in 2" sections. When the first layer is done, go back and do a second layer and then a third. After the top layer is on, brush lightly with one final coating of glue. Place a votive candle inside and set aside to dry. Participants may claim them after fellowship time.

Fellowship

Ideally this program should close with a time of fellowship. Consider offering traditional Halloween party snacks like apples or caramel apples, popcorn, cupcakes, apple cider, or pumpkin desserts. However, your planning team will need to decide how you want your event to flow. Just be sure to include a time of fellowship in your program, whether a full meal or light refreshments.

Optional Activities

The planning team may wish to add a costume flashlight parade to this event. Ahead of time, the team will need to publicize the option of wearing a costume (specify nothing scary or grotesque). Also ask for participants to bring flashlights. After fellowship time, have participants walk around the church property or through the neighborhood surrounding the church carrying their flashlights so that they are shining like lights in the darkness.

A second option, particularly if your church is located in a residential neighborhood, is to have volunteers out in front of the church on Halloween giving away a special church treat (treat with a Bible passage attached). Suggestions might be goldfish crackers with Matthew 4:18-25 or sunflower seeds with Matthew 13:1-23 or chocolate coins with Luke 15:8-10. Or order extra glow sticks and hand out glow sticks with Ephesians 5:8-9. Recruit your volunteers from your Bright Night participants. Maybe being a trick-or-treat greeter on Halloween can be their "next step" in shining brightly for God.

CHAPTER 25

October
Dia de los Muertos

Program Focus: A Hispanic cultural celebration of life and death

Key Verse: "Honor your father and your mother, as long as the LORD your God commanded you, so that your days may be long and that it may go well with you in the land that the LORD your God is giving you" (Deuteronomy 5:16 NRSV).

Purpose:
a. To understand the faith roots of a Hispanic cultural/religious tradition
b. To remember and honor loved ones and church members who have died
c. To praise God who gives us comfort and strength in times of loss and sadness

Leader Background

Dia de los Muertos (Day of the Dead) is a little like a Mexican Halloween. Like the U.S. holiday, it has religious roots in both pagan and Christian traditions, and also like Halloween, Dia de los Muertos is partly celebrated in dark and morbid ways that dishonor those religious origins. However, for thousands of years, the native Mexican Indian cultures, particularly the Aztecs, had celebrated the cycle of life and death, honoring those who have died through a month-long festival that took place in August. When the conquistadors arrived from Spain in the 1500s, they brought with them their Catholic rituals and traditions. To the Spaniards, the native people's Day of the Dead festival seemed pagan and barbaric, as the celebrations seemed to focus on dark and devilish death imagery. Since Pope Gregory IV had already established November 1 as All Saints Day and November 2 had by then become All Souls Day, the Spaniards did their best to convert the Mexican traditions to Christian ones and moved the Dia de los Muertos celebrations to early November.

Yet moving the date did not change the focus of the Dia de los Muertos celebrations; the focus simply became more Christian as more native Mexican and Central American residents assimilated the immigrant culture. Dia de los Muertos evolved into a three-day celebration that honors deceased friends and relatives and gives living family members a way to purposefully remember their loved ones. Most of October is spent preparing for the holiday, with families cooking special foods, building a home altar to house pictures of the loved ones (as well as the crucifix), and harvesting or purchasing flowers to decorate the graves. On October 31 it is believed that the angelitos (spirits of the children who have died) visit first. On November 1 All Souls Day is celebrated by relatives traveling from house to house, bringing a gift for each home altar and sharing in the food the host family has prepared. In many towns church bells ring every hour, letting the people know that the adult spirits are on their way home. On November 2 families go to church in the morning. Later in the afternoon the church bells stop ringing, signaling that the spirits have departed. The families then pack up their special foods and their flowers and gifts and take them to the cemeteries where they decorate the graves and have a picnic with other friends and neighbors while they keep their dead relatives company.

While these traditions may seem strange to many Americans, the Dia de los Muertos celebration is about remembering and honoring loved ones who have died, and there is nothing strange about that. This program will engage participants in Hispanic culture while drawing parallels to their own Christian faith.

Note: During the publicity/registration phase of this event, the planning team should request that participants bring with them photos of friends and loved ones who have died. The team should also ask for donations of inexpensive bunches of flowers. These can be brought to the event and will be used for worship. In addition, the planning team may want to invite a special guest speaker who celebrates Dia de los Muertos to be part of Station 1 to share his or her experiences.

Faith Stations

Station 1. Dia de los Muertos

What You'll Need

Volunteers: station host, guest speaker or picture book on Dia de los Muertos (e.g., *Day of the Dead* by Tony Johnston, Harcourt Brace, 1997)

Skull cookie supplies (skull-shaped or round sugar cookies, white frosting, black decorator icing, plastic knives, paper plates)

Globe

White construction paper cut into strips 1/2" x 3", 1/2" x 4", 2" x 8", 1/4" x 3")

White construction paper ovals (about 3" long)

Brads

Glue sticks

The station host should welcome participants and invite them to gather in a semicircle. Explain that participants will be learning about a Hispanic holiday that has roots in Christianity, and then give some of the Dia de los Muertos information from the Leader Background. If a special guest speaker will be sharing Dia de los Muertos traditions with the group, introduce him or her and let the speaker begin. If not using a guest speaker, read the Dia de los Muertos picture book to the group.

After the story, invite participants over to the tables to work on one or both crafts. Explain that Dia de los Muertos celebrations poke fun and make light of death while at the same time honoring loved ones and friends who have died. Part of the fun is to enjoy sweet treats shaped like skulls or to make skeleton decorations. Participants can choose to decorate a sugar cookie with white frosting and use black decorator icing to create a skull face and/or they can make paper skeletons.

To make the paper skeleton, start with a 2" x 8" strip. Use the brads to join two 3" arm strips together to make a jointed arm. Attach to the body with a brad and repeat for the opposite side. Then use brads to join two 4" leg strips together to make a jointed leg. Attach to the body with a brad and repeat for the opposite side. Decorate the skull head and attach to body with a brad. Then take five or six 1/4" strips and glue horizontally across the body for ribs.

Station 2. Butterflies

What You'll Need

Volunteer: station host

Sheets of white paper towel

Watercolor paints and brushes

Black construction paper

Sheets of wax paper

1/2" squares of orange and black tissue paper

Glue sticks

Yarn or ribbon

Scissors

Hole punch

Wire clothes hangers

The Very Hungry Caterpillar by Eric Carle (Penguin Group, 1994)

The station host should welcome participants and invite them to sit in a semicircle. Ask the group what they know about butterflies. If the group does not offer the information, remind them that butterflies start out as caterpillars that spin cocoons, which allow them to become new creations—butterflies. Explain to the group that butterflies have a connection to Dia de los Muertos celebrations for two reasons. First, ancient Aztec warriors believed that after warriors died, they came back as butterflies or hummingbirds. Second, the Monarch butterfly migrates back to its homeland in Mexico and Central America at the same time as the Day of the Dead celebrations each year. The butterflies are believed to be the spirits of loved ones returning from the dead as new creations. In addition, Christians often use the butterfly as a symbol of new life. You may also share 2 Corinthians 5:17, which talks about becoming a new creation in Christ.

Next, read *The Very Hungry Caterpillar*. After the story, ask participants to break into small groups and answer the following questions:

1. The hungry caterpillar stuffs himself full of junk food before going into his cocoon. What kind of junk food do we feed our spirits?

2. How do you think the caterpillar felt when he discovered that he had transformed into a beautiful butterfly?

3. How does Jesus help us transform and become new creations?

After 5–10 minutes of discussion, invite participants to move to the worktables to make butterflies. They can make one or both styles depending on time.

Paper Towel Tie-Dye Butterflies

1. Take 1 sheet of paper towel, fold in half, and cut away from the fold, making a large B. When the B is opened, it should look like a butterfly shape.

2. Use the water color paints to dab spots of color on the butterfly. Work slowly with a minimal amount of water so that the towel does not get saturated. Let the color spread before adding a new color.

Tissue Paper Monarch Butterflies

1. Take 1 sheet of black construction paper, fold in half, and cut away from the fold, making a large B. Then, while still folded, cut out an arch in each loop of the B so that you are left with a 1" black butterfly frame.

2. Run a glue stick over the frame and lay a sheet of wax paper over the frame. Trim off any excess wax paper.

3. Fill in the butterfly frame by gluing on 1/2" squares of orange and black tissue paper.

4. To hang the butterflies, punch a hole in the top of the frame and run a length of ribbon or yarn through it. Multiple butterflies can be hung from wire hangers and used as decorations in worship.

Station 3. Worship Prep

What You'll Need

Volunteer: station host

Family Memories handout

Pens

Assorted candles

Photos and flowers (brought by participants)

Inexpensive white or cream-colored tablecloth

Fabric markers

Note: The planning team will need to set up a family altar in the worship area with an 8' table. Participants will place photos of family members and friends who have died on the altar, along with flowers and candles. The candles can be lit before worship. Participants should also leave the Family Memories handouts by the photos so the worship leader has easy access to names.

Ahead of time, the planning team should create the Family Memories handout. It should have a blank for the name of a loved one or friend who has died along with 5 blank lines. Each handout can have space for 3 or 4 names.

The host should welcome participants and invite them to gather at the worktables. Ask participants to place the photos they brought on the table and then work on completing the Family Memories handout using the person in the photo (participants may also include other family members or friends whose photos are not present). The deceased person's name goes at the top of the list. The 5 blank lines below are space to write 5 things they remember, love, or admire about the person. Each person in a family group can make their own list, or families can work together to complete the handout. After 10 minutes, ask participants to share the information on their handout with their table group.

When participants finish discussing, they can bring their handouts, along with any photos and flowers to the special family altar in the worship area. They may also bring a candle for the altar. The altar cloth should be on the table already. Participants can add with fabric markers the names of loved ones, friends, or church members who have died to the altar cloth and then place the handouts, photos, flowers, and candles (unlit) on the altar. Names of deceased family members and friends will be read from the handouts and lifted up in prayers of remembrance and thanksgiving during worship. While these traditions may seem strangely like ancestor worship to many U.S. Christians, Dia de los Muertos celebrations are essentially opportunities to remember and honor loved ones who have died, and there is nothing strange about that. Feel free to adapt this portion of the program so that it fits with your own church culture and worship style.

Worship

Opening Song(s): Open your time together with 3–5 songs of praise and worship that support the theme of honoring and remembering our friends and loved ones. Possibilities include "For All the Saints," "Shall We Gather at the River," "When the Saints Go Marching In," "As for Me and My House," "Heirlooms."

Scripture Reading: Psalm 78:1-8

Time of Prayer: The worship leader should move to the altar and read the names from the Family Memories handouts, giving thanks for these people. The planning team may also want to provide the names of church members who have died in the past year.

Closing Song: "Bind Us Together"

Fellowship

Ideally this program closes with a time of fellowship over a full meal with a Mexican theme, which could include tamales and pan de muerto; however, your team will need to decide how you want your event to flow. Do you want to start with a meal, then go to the faith stations, and close with worship? Or do you want to open with worship, go to the faith stations, and end with dessert? Each event can be tailored to your group's needs and time constraints. Just be sure to include a time of fellowship in your program, whether a full meal or light refreshments.

CHAPTER 26

November
Spiritual Gifts

Leader Background

In Malcolm Shotwell's book *Creative Programs for the Church Year* (Judson Press, 1985), Shotwell defines the Holy Spirit as "God, present and at work within and through us and others who are willing to receive this gift." He then expands this definition to say, "The Holy Spirit is God and Jesus at work in our day enabling us to have spiritual birth and life, revealing truth about God and leading us into all truth; glorifying Jesus as his spokesman; becoming our eternal Helper with us and in us; teaching, producing His fruit in our lives, and empowering us to witness" (p. 79). The bottom line is that the Holy Spirit breathes godly life into us so that we might breathe out and share the breath of heaven with the world.

How we do that is with the spiritual gifts God has given to each person. No matter how young or old we are, God has created his children to carry out his work in the world and build up the body of Christ. This program will help participants explore the identity of the Holy Spirit with a focus on identifying spiritual gifts and growing the fruit of the Spirit to use in service to God.

Program Focus: Using and building up your spiritual gifts

Key Verses: "Now there are varieties of gifts, but the same Spirit; and there are varieties of services, but the same Lord; and there are varieties of activities, but it is the same God who activates all of them in everyone. To each is given the manifestation of the Spirit for the common good" (1 Corinthians 12:4-6 NRSV).

Purpose:
a. To identify at least one spiritual gift per participant
b. To explore ways to use different spiritual gifts as part of Christian stewardship (time and talent, as well as treasure)
c. To create a personal "next step" to put a gift to use

Faith Stations

Station 1. Spiritual Gifts

What You'll Need

Volunteer: station host

Bibles

Large cardboard box with removable lid wrapped like a present

15 smaller wrapped boxes with removable lids each filled with 6 pieces of wrapped candy (e.g., mini candy bars, Tootsie Rolls, or sticks of gum) with a preprinted, self-stick address label on the wrapper listing a spiritual gift (apostles, prophets, evangelists, pastors, teachers, service, wisdom, knowledge, faith, healing, miracles, public speaking, discernment, speaking in tongues [other languages], explaining what is said in tongues)

Sheet of mural paper with the outline of a person drawn on it (about 6' tall)

3 sets of 4 sheets of poster board each with a different symbol drawn at the top (a heart, a brain/head, a hand, a foot)

Markers

The station host should welcome participants and invite them to gather in a semicircle. Ask the group if they like to receive presents. Take out the big wrapped box and ask for a volunteer to open it. Then continue to ask for volunteers to pull out the smaller boxes one at a time and open them. Either the volunteer or the host can read the card. The volunteer may take a piece of candy from the box plus one to share with another group member. The host should ask people to save their wrappers.

When all the boxes have been opened, ask:

1. Does anyone know what kind of gifts we found in the boxes? (spiritual gifts)

2. The Bible tells us it is the Spirit who gives us our gifts, but what do you think happens when we use our gifts and share our God-given talents with others?

Ask participants to break into groups of 8 and read together 1 Corinthians 12:1-19. After giving the groups a chance to read, repeat question 2 and ask them how this passage answers that question. After a few minutes of group discussion, display the 4 posters: head, heart, hand, and foot. Tell participants to look at the candy wrappers labeled with the spiritual gifts and call out gifts that seem to relate to each part of the body of Christ.

The head gifts are:

1. prophets
2. pastors
3. teachers
4. wisdom
5. knowledge
6. public speaking
7. discerning
8. speaking in tongues (other languages)
9. explaining what is said in tongues

Heart gifts are:

1. faith
2. healing
3. miracles

A hand gift is:

1. serving

Foot gifts are:

1. apostles
2. evangelists

Once the gifts are categorized, ask the group to brainstorm specific examples of/uses for that type of gift and write those on the posters. Some examples might include:

1. Head gift/teaching/being a Sunday school teacher
2. Heart gift/healing/being a doctor or nurse
3. Hand gift/serving/using carpentry skills to repair the church or build a home for someone in need
4. Foot gift/evangelist/taking God's Word into another country

After a list of examples is created on the posters, ask participants to form groups of 8 and try to identify at least one spiritual gift for each person in their group. Adults should help children think about things they are good at and how that might be evidence of a developing spiritual gift (e.g., helping a friend with homework or a new sports skill might illustrate the gift of teaching). As soon as participants have identified a spiritual gift, they can come up to the body outline and write their name and gift in that area of the body, filling in the arms and legs if needed.

Station 2. Fruit of the Spirit Salad

What You'll Need

Volunteer: station host

Fruit for fruit salad (see below)

Disposable plastic bowls

Forks

Packages of fruit snacks to give as prizes

Ahead of time, the planning team should prepare the Fruit of the Spirit Salad ingredients by cutting up the following fruits (fresh, canned, or frozen), placing them in serving bowls, and labeling them with a name card: love—strawberry, joy—oranges, peace—grapes, patience—pineapple, kindness—apple, goodness—peach, faithfulness—pear, humility—blueberry, and self-control—banana. It will work best if the station area is set up with multiple tables for small group time, each with a complete set of fruit bowls and serving spoons. Each table will also need participant bowls and forks.

The station host should welcome participants and invite them to sit in a semicircle. Ask the group if they can list the fruit of the Spirit. Award a package of fruit snacks if anyone can name all nine. Then read Galatians 5:22-25 and explain that the Spirit gives us spiritual gifts to use in service to God. However, we are also able to grow the fruit of the Spirit in our hearts when we let the Spirit be at work in us. Ask participants to break into groups of 4–5 and facilitate regroupings so that singles and older adults are mixed with family groups.

Groups should then move to the tables. Explain that a table leader needs to read the card in front of each bowl of fruit and ask group members to decide if they possess that fruit of the Spirit. If yes, they may

take a piece of that fruit and add it to their own bowl. They also need to share one way they demonstrate that fruit of the Spirit. After the group has decided which fruits they already exhibit, the table leader should go around the group again and ask which fruits they need to grow in their hearts. Participants should try to give an example of how they would begin to demonstrate this fruit of the Spirit.

Adults should help children understand this question (e.g., if a child needs to grow patience, she can try counting to 10 and offering to share instead of yelling at her sibling for taking her toy without asking). As participants offer to work on different fruits, they may add those to their bowl. When finished with discussion, groups can say a prayer of thanksgiving and eat their fruit salad. Leftover fruit can be served during fellowship time.

Station 3. Spirit Means Breath (Games)

What You'll Need

Volunteer: station host

5"–7" round balloons (1 per person)

Bags of 100 mini water balloons (1 bag per team of 8)

3 to 4 Ping-Pong balls

2 8' lengths of gutter

Straws (1 per person)

Wind-theme prizes (optional; such as pinwheels, flags, kites, etc.)

Rolls of masking tape (1 per team)

The host should gather the group and explain that in Hebrew, the word used for Spirit of God is *ruach*. In Greek the word is *pneuma*. As Malcolm Shotwell writes:

> Both words referred to "wind" (free), "breath" (life), and "spirit" (power/mystery). The Spirit of God is life-giving breath without which we remain spiritually inert. It is the mysterious wind that we cannot manufacture (as Nicodemus was reminded by Jesus in John 3:8). The wind is also powerful. Notions of power and mystery mark much of the teaching of Old and New Testament alike when they treat "the Spirit of God." (*Creative Programs for the Church Year* [Judson Press, 1985], 79)

Participants will be playing several games at this station that involve breath and breathing.

November | American Indian Heritage Month

Using your denominational/organizational resources or personal contacts, find a sister church located on an American Indian reservation or with a large American Indian population. The planning team should contact the church leaders to make sure this program is feasible. Early in the month, host an intergenerational night where stations will include participants retelling favorite Bible stories, giving a tour of the church, explaining its history, and worshiping together. Videotape the entire evening and convert the tape to a DVD. The planning team should ask the sister church to do the same. DVDs should be exchanged and a second intergenerational program held to view the DVD.

Note: The planning team should ship the video equipment to the sister church if necessary, as well as arrange for its return with the footage.

The planning team can also request that the sister church send examples or titles of American Indian legends, as well as samples of or directions for simple, authentic crafts. The stories can be shared and the crafts made at this second program. Depending on the financial needs of the sister church, the planning team may wish to take up a special offering during worship to send to the other church and/or may set up a pen pal program with members of the sister church.

For a wide variety of ideas that can be converted to station content, visit the following websites:

- www.edgateteam.net/Lessons/american_indian_heritage.htm
- www.smithsonianeducation.org/educators/resource_library/american_indian_resources.html
- www.tolatsga.org/Compacts.html

Ping-Pong Relay

Ahead of time, the host should set up the 2 lengths of gutter on a long table. Depending on the size of the group, the host could set up additional tables to make the teams smaller and/or could use building blocks to create channels for the race if gutter sections are unavailable. Each team will need 1 Ping-Pong ball, and each person will need 1 straw.

Half of the teams line up behind the starting end of the table and have to use the straw to blow on the ball to move it to the opposite end of the table. The other half of the teams will be waiting and will use their straws to move it back to the starting end. Repeat this process until the first team works through all their members and wins the challenge. Award small prizes if desired.

Balloon Relay

Ahead of time the host should mark a starting and finish line across the width of the room about 25'–40' apart, depending on the size of the group.

Create teams of 6 people, mixing up family groups if possible to maximize fellowship opportunities. Let adults know that they can help children. Each person should receive 1 round balloon. On the signal, the first person will blow up the balloon and then aim it toward the finish line and let go. The first person and second person must go to the spot where it lands. The first person will pick up the balloon and stay put while the second person blows up his or her balloon, aims it, and lets go. The second and third team members move to the landing spot of the second balloon. The second person now picks up the balloon and stays put while the third person repeats the process with the fourth team member being added, and so on.

The goal is to be the first team to cross the finish line. If the team runs out of members before reaching the finish line, the first person can continue the path, then the second, etc.

Filled with the Holy Spirit

This game is similar to the mummy toilet paper wrap game except that the chosen team member is covered with balloons instead of toilet paper. The host divides the group into teams of 8, and each team chooses 1 member to be "It." On the signal, "It"'s team members will begin blowing up the little balloons and taping them onto "It." The goal is to get "It" completely covered in balloons. (Hint: the smaller the "It," the easier the work for the team!) The first team to get their "It" filled with the Holy Spirit balloons wins.

Worship

Opening Song(s): Open your time together with 3–5 songs of praise and worship that support the theme of the Holy Spirit. Possibilities include "Spirit," "Here I Am, Lord," "Spirit of the Living God," "From the Inside Out," "Breathe on Me," "Come, Holy Spirit."

Scripture Reading: John 14:25-26 and Ephesians 4:1-13

Note: After the Scripture reading the worship leader invites the worshipers to take an index card and write one specific "next step" they're going to take to use their spiritual gift. Play a song to give people a few minutes to think and write. Adults should help children as needed. Then have ushers collect the "offerings" and bring them to the front of the worship area.

Time of Prayer: The worship leader holds up the body of Christ spiritual gifts mural that was made in Station 1 and thanks God for blessing the worshipers with these spiritual gifts. Then the worship leader acknowledges participants' offerings of "next steps" in using their spiritual gifts and asks God to continue to equip and encourage them as they minister in God's name.

Closing Song: "Simple Gifts" or "Come and Fill This Place"

Fellowship

Ideally this program should close with a time of fellowship. The leftover fruit from the Fruit of the Spirit activity can be served. Or, if weather permits, consider doing a bonfire for fellowship time (to connect with the fire symbolism of the Holy Spirit) and serve campfire snacks: s'mores, hot dogs, apple cider, hot cocoa. Either way, each event can be tailored to your group's needs and time constraints. Just be sure to include a time of fellowship in your program, whether a full meal or light refreshments.

November | Veteran's Day

Plan an intergenerational event that looks at famous soldiers in the Bible (e.g., David, Gideon, Joshua). Invite veterans from within the church and the larger community to help tell these stories. Prepare a program of patriotic music to be sung or played in honor of the veterans. Make an American flag craft. Invite the veterans to share stories of how their faith carried them through difficult times (see sample program at www.forallgenerations.com).

CHAPTER 27

November
True Thanksgiving

Leader Background

While the Pilgrims and the Wampanoag Indians did celebrate a harvest feast together in 1621, that original feast was never repeated. That feast also featured games, singing, and dancing, elements not included by the Pilgrims in a true religious "thanksgiving" celebration. In addition, it was three days long and celebrated sometime between the end of September and mid-November.

In 1817 New York State adopted a Thanksgiving Day custom, and by the mid-1800s, many other states had followed New York's lead. In 1863 President Abraham Lincoln set aside the last Thursday in November as a day of thanksgiving, which continued because of the Thanksgiving proclamation issued by each subsequent president. Finally, in 1939 President Franklin D. Roosevelt declared the fourth Thursday in November as Thanksgiving. This date was approved by Congress in 1941.

Sadly, our highly commercialized Thanksgiving holiday often does little to embody the original worshipful spirit of the Pilgrims, who really knew a thing or two about thanking God. This program will help participants work on acknowledging the gifts that God has given and on truly giving thanks for all that God is and all that God does in their lives.

Program Focus: Learning to be actively grateful on a daily basis

Key Verse: "Bless the LORD, O my soul, and all that is within me, bless his holy name" (Psalm 103:1 NRSV).

Purpose:

a. To introduce/reintroduce biblical stories of Thanksgiving: Jacob and Esau's reconciliation, Ruth, and Paul (I give thanks for you)

b. To acknowledge that all we have comes from God and identify those things we are thankful for

c. To celebrate God's goodness and learn how to give thanks when life isn't so joyful

Worship

Opening Song(s): Open your time together with 3–5 songs of praise and worship that reflect thankfulness for our blessings from God. Possibilities include "We Gather Together," "All Creatures of Our God and King," "Come, You Thankful People, Come," "Now Thank We All Our God," "Give Thanks," "I Will Give Thanks," "O Give Thanks."

Scripture Reading: Philippians 4:4-7

Responsive Reading: Psalm 103 (read responsively, alternating verses between leader and people)

Time of Prayer: The worship leader should ask for worshipers to lift up things for which they are thankful. The leader can also pray with a focus on gratefulness in all circumstances.

Closing Song: "The Doxology"

Faith Stations

Station 1. The Shema

What You'll Need

Volunteer: station host

Toothpicks

Strips of brown paper (construction paper or old grocery bags) cut into 2" x 5" pieces

Small cardboard jewelry box with lid for each family unit (available at craft stores)

Glue sticks and/or craft glue

Craft paint

Glitter

Markers

Buttons, sequins, or craft jewels

The host should welcome participants to the station and invite them to sit at the worktables. Explain that they will be making a Shema. The Shema was a piece of Scripture from the Old Testament that our Bible ancestors kept on the doorposts of their homes. The words reminded people that God was their creator and that God was the only one whom they should worship and praise—everyday! Every time they went in and out of their homes, they saw the special little box that held the Shema and knew the words should guide their lives.

Read Deuteronomy 6:4-9 and ask groups to discuss the following questions with the other people at their tables:

1. What were the special instructions God gave his people in this passage?

2. How did God say they were supposed to keep reminding themselves of these words?

3. Do you have any God words written on your heart? Would you share the verse with your table group?

4. How can learning and remembering these words help us practice gratefulness to God?

When groups have finished discussing, explain the Shema craft.

For each individual project you will need 2 toothpicks, a strip of scroll paper, a small box with lid, a pen, decorating supplies, and glue. Participants can make household or individual boxes.

Shema Directions

1. Put a line of glue at the top and bottom of the scroll paper.

2. Lay a toothpick on the glue at both ends and roll up a few times to secure.

3. Write the Shema verse on the scroll: "Hear, O Israel: The LORD is our God, the LORD alone. You shall love the LORD your God with all your heart, and with all your soul, and with all your might" (Deuteronomy 6:4-5 NRSV).

4. Decorate your Shema box as desired.

5. When glue is dry, roll up your scroll and place it inside the Shema box. Keep your box near the main doorway of your home.

Station 2: Campfire Stories

What You'll Need

Volunteer: station host, 2 storytellers

Logs

Red, yellow, and orange tissue paper

Sheets of cellophane

Robes

Ties for Bible storytellers (3, including the host)

Ahead of time, build a pretend fire with the real logs; red, yellow, and orange tissue paper; and cellophane. The host should welcome participants and gather them around the fire to hear the stories of Jacob and Esau (told by Jacob), Ruth, and Paul.

Note: Ahead of time, the storytellers should read the following passages to prepare for their storytelling roles. The planning team may also want to provide them with copies of additional background materials so they are comfortable telling their character's story, ideally in the first person.

Jacob and Esau

- The backstory: a brother lies, cheats, and steals (Genesis 27).

- Nevertheless, that brother, Jacob, is blessed by God (Genesis 28–31).

- Jacob prepares to meet his long-lost brother, Esau (Genesis 32).

- Jacob gives thanks to God and reconciles with Esau (Genesis 33).

The storyteller's focus is on Jacob's gratefulness to God for such a blessed life (in spite of the sins he has committed and mistakes he has made along the way), which he shares when he reunites with Esau in chapter 33. However, the storyteller will need to know the backstory to see how Jacob came to this grateful response.

Ruth

- The story (Ruth 1–4).

The storyteller's focus is on Ruth's gratefulness to Naomi for making her part of the family when she could have sent her packing after Ruth's first husband died, as well as her gratefulness to Boaz for showing her kindness and marrying her, which led to her becoming part of the family of Jesus.

Paul

- The backstory (Acts 9:1-22): Paul becomes a follower of Jesus.

- Paul's prayers of thanksgiving (Romans 1:8-15; 1 Corinthians 1:4-9; Ephesians 1:15-23; Philippians 1:2-11).

The storyteller's focus is on the fact that Paul's response to Jesus' call is to follow him (just as our grateful response to Jesus' gift of himself is to follow and serve only him), as well as on Paul's emphasis on thanksgiving for the believers. He frequently starts his letters with a message to the believers telling them how thankful he is for them and their faithfulness or desire to serve. What an encouraging message for us to hear!

Note: Each storyteller should spend about 5 minutes telling his or her story and then asking and answering any questions the group has.

Station 3: Reaching Out to Others

What You'll Need

Volunteer: station host

Small empty cardboard oatmeal canisters with lids or cereal boxes with closing flaps intact

White paper to wrap around canisters or boxes

Glue

Stickers or stamps with mission or helping themes

Markers

Scissors

Mission posters (see below)

Dried corn kernels (enough for 5 per participant)

The planning team will need to do some advance work. In August or September get a list from your church leaders of all the places your mission money goes. Contact these organizations and ask them to send you annual reports and brochures explaining their programs and services. Make posters for this program highlighting the different ways the church's mission offerings are at work in God's world. In addition to your church's recipients, locate area charities and get similar information from them. Arrange these posters around your work area, which will have all the supplies ready for participants to make their own mission banks.

The host should welcome participants and invite them to sit at the worktables. Explain that another way we can show God how grateful we are for all that we have is to share our riches with others. This includes time, talent, and money. Not only do offerings and volunteer time help a church, but they also serve as God's hands and heart out in the world. Ask participants to look at the posters around the room to see where the church's mission offerings go and how they help God's people.

Ask the group, "Do you support any particular missions or ministry programs at home? If yes, what are they?"

Invite participants to go around the room and look at the mission posters and information. Participants should make a list of missions they might like to support. When they are ready, each household can make a "giving thanks" mission bank. Use it to collect offerings for one of the featured missions, a Sunday school mission project, or another mission program of the family's choosing.

Mission Bank Directions

1. Cut the white paper to fit your container and decorate with a helping or giving theme.

2. Write the words from 1 Timothy 6:18-19 on the cover and glue to the container. Make sure the lid or box top flaps have an opening cut for money deposits.

3. Before you begin to decorate your bank, give each person 5 dried kernels of corn. Go around your table group and ask each person to share five things for which he or she is grateful this year. After the person shares, he or she can glue the kernels to the bank. This "five kernels" tradition dates back to the early 1600s when only five kernels of corn were given to each person in the pilgrims' settlement for their daily food. Later, people placed five kernels of corn at their table each Thanksgiving Day to remind them of how much they had to be grateful for.[1]

4. Keep your bank in a central place at home so you will remember to contribute to it regularly and share your riches. This is one way we show God how grateful we are for the blessings he gives us.

November | National Adoption Awareness Month

Host an intergenerational program centered on Ephesians 1:5 ("He destined us for adoption as his children through Jesus Christ, according to the good pleasure of his will" [NRSV]). Invite adoptive families to come share their stories. Have a storyteller recreate the story of Naomi, Ruth, and Boaz and explore Ruth's adoptive relationship to Naomi and the Davidic line. Create a mural-sized church family tree that shows generations of families who belong to the church, as well as members who joined because of the invitation of a friend.

For more background information and ideas visit the following websites:

• www.adoptivefamilies.com/pdf/ 2007calendar.pdf

• national-adoption-month.adoption.com

• www.nationaladoptionawarenessmonth .com/celebrate.html

Fellowship

Ideally, this program should close with a time of fellowship; however, your planning team may want to consider the extension activities below in lieu of traditional fellowship offerings. Either way, the event can be tailored to your group's needs and time constraints. Just be sure to include a time of fellowship in your program, whether it features a full meal or light refreshments.

Extension Activities

To help participants identify with the bounty of their blessings, especially compared to some brothers and sisters elsewhere in the country or in the world, the planning team may want to consider holding a "Poverty Supper" in lieu of the normal meal. Participants would instead be served a bowl of broth, 2 crackers, and a cup of coffee, tea, or lemonade. A free-will offering could be collected that would represent what participants would have paid for a meal in a restaurant.[2]

If your intergenerational events have been ending simply with refreshments and not a full meal, consider not serving any treats and encourage participants to go home and go to bed without a snack, again giving thanks for the bounty of their blessings.

Notes

1. Adapted from Malcolm Shotwell, *Creative Programs for the Church Year* (Valley Forge, PA: Judson Press, 1985), 16.

2. Adapted from Shotwell, 15–16.

CHAPTER 28

December
Las Posadas

Leader background

Drawing on the vibrancy of the Mexican culture, a Las Posadas (The Inns) celebration can enhance the wonder and joy of Advent. Traditionally, participants recreate Joseph's and Mary's trip to Bethlehem by traveling parade-style from *posada* to *posada* (inn to inn) on the nine nights preceding Christmas. However, this Las Posadas program is designed as a one-night adventure during which participants travel room to room in your church seeking shelter for the holy family. At each room, they have a conversation with the innkeeper, who shares part of the Christmas story. The journey concludes with all travelers meeting for worship in the sanctuary where the Christ child lies in the manger. You can share this explanation with your participants before sending them on their journey.

Fellowship

Ideally this program begins with a Mexican-style dinner. Ahead of time, the planning team will either need to make arrangements to cater this meal or have an advance sign-up for specific food items. A suggested menu is tacos (shells with seasoned ground beef or chicken, lettuce, tomato, cheese, hot sauce, onion, etc.), refried beans, nacho chips with cheese sauce and salsa, sliced oranges, and coffee, tea, and milk. For more variety you could also add tamales to this menu (available frozen at most grocery stores). Also check out the ethnic food aisle of your store and provide a sampling of Mexican sodas for drinks.

If you have a Spanish speaker in your group, ask him or her to lead grace before dinner. If not, the planning team can also search the Internet or the library for a simple Spanish grace to say. Dessert can be served following the closing worship service.

Program Focus: Celebrating Advent in the Hispanic faith tradition

Key Verse: "The people who walked in darkness have seen a great light; those living in a land of deep darkness—on them light has shined" (Isaiah 9:2 NRSV).

Purpose:
a. To relive the holy family's journey to Bethlehem
b. To better understand our spiritual journey during Advent
c. To create a "next step" in our own faith journeys during Advent

Faith Stations

Note: Ahead of time, the planning team will need to recruit one teen or adult to play the innkeeper at each of the five inn sites plus one worship leader and one instrumentalist.

What You'll Need

Station host, 1 teen or adult to play the innkeeper at each of the 5 inn sites, worship leader, instrumentalist

5 separate sites in your church for the inns

Sign marking each inn

Candles to light each inn

Battery-powered candles for travelers to carry with them (or 1 for the leader in each group if your church does not own these; could also use flashlights and/or ask people to bring their own flashlights)

Robe or tunic costumes for the innkeepers (and participants if desired)

Copies of scripts for all innkeepers and participants

After dinner, the station host should divide participants into smaller groups of 10–20 people, making sure to combine singles, older adults, and families. Each group will start with Inn 1, so you will need to stagger your departure times to about every 7 minutes. If your church program space is large and spread out, you can increase the size of your groups. For extremely large gatherings, set up 2 or more complete Las Posadas routes to accommodate the travelers. Use outdoor spaces, if possible, for variety.

For the groups not leaving immediately (and those returning first), have a few activities available to keep them occupied. The host can facilitate these as needed.

• Put on Christmas music and let people make cards.

• Arrange chairs in a large circle (1 for each person, minus 1) and play No Room in the Inn. Assign each person to be Joseph, Mary, or the innkeeper. "It" stands in the middle and calls one of the characters. All people assigned to that character jump up and switch seats. "It" tries to sit in one of the empty seats. Whoever is left without a seat is the new "It." When "It" calls, "No room in the inn," all players must get up and switch seats. Whoever is left without a seat is the new "It." Groups who

departed first or second can play this game when they return to your gathering area.

• Play a Christmas video.

• Set a variety of board games out on the tables.

The host should direct each group to first find Inn 1 and explain that when they arrive, they will read the script in unison. When they finish their visit, they need to find Inn 2 and repeat the process until they've visited all 5 sites. They should return to the gathering area to wait for all groups to finish before proceeding to worship. It will take approximately 30 to 45 minutes for your groups to move through all 5 stations, depending on group size and your inn layout.

Note: The innkeepers should stand in a doorway so that participants are blocked from entering the "inn." If possible, keep the lights off or low throughout your church so that participants are traveling by candlelight (if using the battery-powered candles). Just keep enough lights on for safety, especially in stairways.

Inn 1

Travelers: Hello. Do you have any room at the inn? Joseph and Mary need a place to stay.

Innkeeper: No, I'm sorry. There's no room here. But I have a wonderful story to tell you. Maybe it will give you comfort even though I cannot help you. Isaiah, a prophet in the Old Testament, told this story long before it ever happened. He said, "The people walking in darkness have seen a great light; on those living in the land of the shadow of death a light has dawned" (Isaiah 9:2 NIV).

Travelers: "For to us a child is born, to us a son is given, and the government will be on his shoulders. And he will be called Wonderful Counselor . . ." (Isaiah 9:6 NIV).

Innkeeper: "Mighty God" (Isaiah 9:6 NIV).

Travelers: "Everlasting Father" (Isaiah 9:6 NIV).

Innkeeper: "Prince of Peace. Of the increase of his government and peace there will be no end" (Isaiah 9:7 NIV). Hear the good news! Jesus Christ, our Savior and Messiah, will be born! Go in peace on your journey. Shalom.

Inn 2

Travelers: Hello. Is there any room at this inn? Mary and Joseph need a place to stay. Mary is getting very tired, and her back hurts from riding the donkey.

Innkeeper: Oh, I'm so sorry, but my inn is full. I don't think I can help you this evening, but before you go, let me tell you a special story. It's a happy one that might lift your spirits before you continue on your way. Two thousand years ago, God sent the angel Gabriel to the town of Nazareth in Galilee with a message for a girl named Mary. She was engaged to Joseph, whose great-grandfather 25 times over was King David, who killed the giant Goliath. The angel said, "Greetings, you who are highly favored!" (Luke 1:28 NIV).

Travelers: But we're confused. What did the angel mean?

Innkeeper: The angel told Mary, "Don't be afraid. God is pleased with you and has chosen you to have his Son. His name will be Jesus. He will be great and will be called the Son of God. He will rule the earth forever" (Luke 1:30-33, paraphrase).

Travelers: But we're still confused. How could this happen? Mary wasn't married yet.

Innkeeper: "The Holy Spirit will come down to you, and God's power will come over you," the angel told Mary. "So your child will be called the Holy Son of God. Nothing is impossible for God" (Luke 1:35, 37, paraphrase).

Travelers: Mary was brave. She told the angel, "Here I am, the servant of the Lord. Let it be as you have said" (Luke 1:38, paraphrase).

Innkeeper: Hear the good news! Jesus Christ, the Holy Son of God, will be born to the Virgin Mary. Go in peace now.

Inn 3

Travelers: Hello! Do you have any room at this inn? Mary is going to have a baby, and she is tired of traveling.

Innkeeper: Oh, I am so sorry, but my inn is full. I already have many families staying here. But I can tell you the most beautiful story before you leave. It's a song of praise and thanksgiving. Mary sang it to God to thank God for blessing her with a baby.

Travelers: Mary's baby was going to be Jesus!

Innkeeper: Yes, and here's how she said thank you to God: "My soul glorifies the Lord and my spirit rejoices in God my Savior, for he has been mindful of the humble state of his servant. From now on all generations will call me blessed" (Luke 1:47-48 NIV).

Travelers: "For the Mighty One has done great things for me—holy is his name" (Luke 1:49 NIV).

Innkeeper: "He has performed mighty deeds with his arm. . . . He has filled the hungry with good things but has sent the rich away empty" (Luke 1:51a, 53 NIV).

Travelers: "The Lord made a promise to our ancestors, blessing Abraham and his family forever!" (Luke 1:55, paraphrase).

Innkeeper: And God always keeps his promises. He will keep you safe on your journey and provide for you. Go in peace.

Inn 4

Travelers: Hello, Innkeeper, do you have any room in your inn? It is cold outside, and Mary and Joseph have been traveling many days. Mary is going to have a son, God's Son. She needs a place to lie down and rest.

Innkeeper: No, I'm very sorry, but there is no room in my inn. Bethlehem is very full because of the census. I have no room to spare. But before you move on, let me tell you a story that has an amazing ending. Before Jesus was born, there was a leader named Caesar Augustus who ruled a lot of land and a lot of people. He wanted to know exactly how many people he was in charge of, so he made everyone go back to the town where they were born to be counted in a census. Joseph had to go from Nazareth, where he lived, to the city of Bethlehem, where he was born. He took Mary with him because she was going to be his wife. She was also pregnant with God's Son. While they were in Bethlehem, the time came for Mary to have her baby (Luke 2:1-6, paraphrase).

Travelers: But there is no room at your inn! Where will Mary and Joseph stay?

Innkeeper: Travelers, you must move on. As I said, I have no room here. But don't worry. God will provide for them. Shalom.

Inn 5

Travelers: Hello! Please, do you have room for Joseph and Mary and your inn? They are so tired and weary from traveling, and it's time for Mary to have her baby now. This is a very important and special baby! Please, don't turn them away!

Innkeeper: I'm sorry, but my inn is full. I don't think I can help your friends tonight. Bethlehem is a very small town, and there are not many inns here.

Travelers: But what about Mary and Joseph? How can God treat them this way? Mary is about to have God's Son. He can't be born in a street! Who will help them? Where will they go?

Innkeeper: Do you know what? Maybe I can help after all. If you go out this door, you will find my stable. It is a very simple place where I keep my animals. But it's clean and safe, and there is fresh straw. At least Mary could lie down and rest awhile.

Travelers: Thank you! We are so grateful! Praise be to God!

Note: When all groups have visited all 5 inns, gather them for closing worship. A time of dessert and fellowship can follow worship if that works for your group.

December | Hanging of the Greens

Prepare your church for Advent with a Hanging of the Greens decorating party. Create stations that allow for different elements of decoration (putting up the nativity set, decorating the Christmas trees with chrismons, hanging greenery and lights). During worship, focus on the prophecy of Christ's birth in Isaiah 9.

Worship

Note: Use candlelight for this service and set up an area in the front of the worship space as the stable with straw and a manger with baby Jesus in it. You will need a song sheet with the carol verses or Power-Point slides ready with the lyrics.

Opening Song(s): Use a centering song such as "Sanctuary" or "Spirit of the Living God" or a traditional hymn like "All Praise to Thee, My God, This Night" to prepare worshipers' hearts.

Opening Carols: "O Come, O Come Emmanuel" (verse 1) and "Away in the Manger" (verse 1)

The Journey Continues

The worship leader tells or reads the rest of the Christmas story, beginning with Luke 2:6-29 and Matthew 2:1-12. At the end of the story, share with people that Advent is a journey of preparation to celebrate the coming of Christ and to welcome him into our lives. Ask people to reflect on the journey they made tonight and their journey with Jesus, especially focusing on one step they can take to welcome Jesus more fully into their lives during this busy season. Play a meditative version of "O Come, All Ye Faithful" while they think. When the carol ends, ask if anyone would like to share one way in which they feel closer to Jesus tonight or one thing they will do to draw closer to Jesus during Advent (pray, come to church every Sunday, do an Advent devotion with family, invite a friend to the Christmas Eve worship service, etc.).

Prayers of the People: The worship leader can ask people to lift up joys and concerns and/or can pray with a special focus on setting time aside to draw closer to Jesus.

Collection of the Offering and Doxology: Optional; perhaps dedicated to a special missions project in your area or that your church sponsors.

Closing Carols: "Go Tell It on the Mountain" (verses 1 and 3) and "Joy to the World" (verse 1)

Benediction

CHAPTER 29

December
Kwanzaa

Program Focus: Unity, self-determination, collective work and responsibility, cooperative economics, purpose, creativity, and faith

Key Verses: "I appeal to you therefore, brothers and sisters, by the mercies of God, to present your bodies as a living sacrifice, holy and acceptable to God, which is your spiritual worship. Do not be conformed to this world, but be transformed by the renewing of your minds, so that you may discern what is the will of God—what is good and acceptable and perfect" (Romans 12:1-2 NRSV).

Purpose:
a. To discover the African American holiday of Kwanzaa
b. To explore the seven principles of Kwanzaa and their value in any culture
c. To identify connections between Christian faith and the principles of Kwanzaa

Leader Background

Kwanzaa celebrations were first held in 1966 when Dr. Maulana Karenga created the holiday to help African Americans remember their cultural heritage. Kwanzaa is based on seven principles: unity, self-determination, collective work and responsibility, cooperative economics, purpose, creativity, and faith. It is celebrated for seven days, from December 26 to January 1, each year. Although it is not a Christian holiday, its principles parallel Christian values and biblical teachings. This program will help participants experience African American culture while understanding Kwanzaa from a faith-based perspective.

Worship

Opening Song(s): Open your time together with 3–5 songs of praise and worship that draw on African American musical faith traditions. Possibilities include "Lift Every Voice and Sing," "Siyahamba" ("Marching in the Light of God"), "I'll Fly Away," "We'll Understand It Better By and By," "Go Down Moses," "Through It All."

Scripture Reading: 2 Thessalonians 2:13-15

Responsive Reading

Leader: People of God, Kwanzaa is a time to remember.

People: Let us remember that all we are and all we have comes from God.

Leader: Let us remember *Umoja*, unity.

People: In Ephesians Paul says that there is unity of the spirit in the bonds of peace (4:3).

Leader: Let us remember *Kujichagulia*, self-determination.

People: In Philippians we learn that God is at work in us and we can do all things through Jesus who strengthens us (2:13; 4:13).

Leader: Let us remember *Ujima*, collective work and responsibility.

People: In Acts, at the birth of the Christian church, we hear how the believers gathered together, sharing their possessions, their food, and their lives with one another so that they might be strengthened to go out and share the good news of Jesus Christ with the world (2:44-47).

Leader: Let us remember *Ujamaa*, cooperative economics.

People: In Proverbs 3:9 we hear King Solomon's wisdom, which tells us to honor God with our wealth and with the best of what we produce with our God-given gifts.

Leader: Let us remember *Nia*, purpose.

People: In Isaiah 43:1 God reminds us that he has called us by name and we are his, forgiven of our sins and redeemed to be his workers in this world.

Leader: Let us remember *Kuumba*, creativity.

People: God formed us in his image, and we are fearfully and wonderfully made! May we be as boldly creative as our Creator in all that we are and all that we do (Psalm 139:13-14).

Leader: Let us remember *Imani*, faith.

People: Faith is the assurance of things hoped for, the belief in things not seen (Hebrews 11:1).

Leader: Let us remember our history, our heritage, our culture, our faith. Let us remember that all we are and all we have come from God.

People: And whatever we do, whatever we say, may we do everything in the name of our Lord Jesus, giving thanks to God through him (Colossians 3:17).

Time of Prayer: The worship leader should ask for worshipers to lift up names of family and friends who have been role models for them in sharing their heritage and their faith. The leader can also pray with a focus on asking God to develop the seven principles within his children so that they might better know him, love him, and serve him.

Closing Song: "Kum Bah Yah"

Faith Stations

Station 1. What Is Kwanzaa?

What You'll Need

Volunteer: station host, guest speaker familiar with celebrating Kwanzaa (optional)

Nonfiction picture books about Kwanzaa, such as *The Seven Days of Kwanzaa* by Melrose Cooper (Cartwheel Books, 2007) or *Kwanzaa* by Carol Gnojewski (Enslow, 2004)

Picture books of African or African American folktales, such as *Anansi the Spider, Brer Rabbit,* or *The Seven Spools of Kwanzaa* by Carol Shelf Medearis (Albert Whitman, 2004)

Examples of Kwanzaa symbols (a placemat or tablecloth, fruits and vegetables, a wooden or pewter goblet or chalice, corn, a wooden candle holder, 7 candles [3 green, 3 red, 1 black] and gifts [books or traditional African handicrafts wrapped in bright African colors])

The station host should welcome participants and invite them to gather in a semicircle. If using a guest speaker, introduce this person to the group and have him or her explain Kwanzaa and its traditions and significance for African Americans. If using the picture books, read the picture book to the group. As you read, you can call up volunteers to create a Kwanzaa display using the props listed above (recreate the display for each rotation).

When you are finished reading (or the speaker is finished talking), ask the group these questions:

1. What's something new you learned about Kwanzaa today?

2. What's something that you really like about Kwanzaa?

For the final question, ask participants to break into groups of 6–8 people. Family groups can split up, and you should facilitate mixing singles and older adults with existing families. After groups have had 10 minutes or so to discuss the final question, ask each of the groups to share some of their answers.

3. Dr. Karenga created the Kwanzaa holiday because he wanted to help African Americans remember their history and their traditions. If you could create a holiday, what holiday would you create? What would it celebrate? What would it help people honor or remember?

If there is time left, the host (or guest speaker) can read or tell one of the African folktales or stories.

Station 2. Connections

What You'll Need

Volunteer: station host

7 banner backgrounds (white or tan felt or burlap approximately 42" wide by 72" long; fold the top edge over 2" and sew or hot glue to create a pocket for a dowel rod)

Fabric scraps (ribbon, trim, African fabric remnants, felt squares, etc.)

Fabric paint (bright jewel/glitter tones)

Fabric/craft glue

Miscellaneous decorating items (buttons, beads, etc.)

Scissors

List of Kwanzaa principles and related Bible verses (unity, Ephesians 4:3; self-determination, Philippians 2:13 and 4:13; collective work and responsibility, Acts 2:44-47; cooperative economics, Proverbs 3:9; purpose, Isaiah 43:1; creativity, Psalm 139:13-14; faith, Hebrews 11:1)

Bibles

Fancy scrapbooking paper

Markers

Red, black, and green construction paper

Sample of the Kwanzaa bandera (flag)

Old magazines, greeting cards, calendars, etc.

Ahead of time, the planning team should label each banner background with one of the seven principles with fabric paint or fabric letters.

The host should welcome participants to the station and ask them to gather in a semicircle. Explain that in this session participants will be working on banners that connect the seven principles of Kwanzaa to the Scriptures referenced during worship. Participants can select the principle they want to work on and use the assorted craft supplies to illustrate that

principle on the banner. Somewhere on the banner should also be the Bible verse, either just the citation or the whole passage written out. These banners will be a collective work of all participants from the three rotations.

In addition to the banners, participants can make a Kwanzaa bandera, or flag, to take home. The Kwanzaa flag uses three colors: black to symbolize Africans and African Americans, red to symbolize struggle, and green to symbolize hope for the future. Participants should use construction paper to create the flag. They can then add to the flag drawings or pictures that symbolize their people (family, ethnic group, age group, etc.), their struggles, and their hopes for the future. Families can work on the flags as a group or make them individually. The host should facilitate combining singles and older adults with family groups as needed.

Station 3. Celebrate Kwanzaa!

What You'll Need

Volunteer: station host

Instrument-making supplies

Oatmeal or other cardboard containers with lids, recycled plastic containers with lids, utility buckets (recycled from construction sites or purchased at a home improvement store)

Assorted colors of tissue paper

Glue

Craft paint

Brushes

Permanent markers

Plastic tablecloths

12" sections of 1/2" dowel rods

Aquarium gravel

Sand

Beads and lanyard for making necklaces (jewel-toned pony beads infused with glitter give a richer color)

Multiple sets of the Mancala board game

CD player

CDs of African or African American music

Paper

Pens and pencils

Ahead of time, the station host should start the music so it is playing as guests are entering the station. The station host should welcome participants and explain that this station involves multiple opportunities to celebrate Kwanzaa. Show the group the various activities and let them self-select. They include the following:

Instrument-making

A covered worktable should be set up with a variety of containers with lids, aquarium gravel, sand, dowel rod drumsticks, paint and brushes, permanent markers, tissue paper and glue, etc. Participants can make drums from the lidded containers. They can leave them empty or fill them with varying amounts of sand to change their sound. They can decorate the outside of the containers with sheets of tissue paper, paint, or markers.

Drums can also be made by turning the plastic utility buckets upside down and drumming on the top with the drumsticks. These can be decorated by gluing on sheets of tissue paper.

Shakers can be made by filling the lidded containers with varying amounts of aquarium gravel or sand. They can be decorated with paint, permanent markers, or tissue paper.

Necklaces

Another worktable should be set up with beading lanyard, scissors, and an assortment of beads. Participants can string necklaces for themselves or to give as gifts.

Mancala

A third table area can provide multiple sets of the board game Mancala. This is a traditional African game for two players of nearly any age. Mancala boards can also be made ahead by the planning team. See the instructions in *Kwanzaa* by Carol Gnojewski (Enslow, 2004), or search the Internet for "Mancala instructions."

Fellowship

Ideally this program closes with a time of fellowship over a full meal. If choosing to do a full meal, the *karuma* is a good model to follow. It is a traditional harvest feast attended by many people. Families typically prepare and bring their favorite recipes to share potluck style. The planning team may also want to suggest some menu items that reflect African or African American foods, such as greens, sweet potatoes, jambalaya, Hoppin' John, plantains, or okra. However, your team will need to decide how you want your event to flow. Do you want to start with a meal, then go to the faith stations, and close with worship? Or do you want to open with worship, go to the faith stations, and end with punch and cookies? Each event can be tailored to your group's needs and time constraints. Just be sure to include a time of fellowship in your program, whether a full meal or light refreshments.

CHAPTER 30

December
First Night

Leader Background

Since 1976 cities around the globe have been hosting First Night celebrations, which are alcohol-free, community-wide New Year's Eve parties. Originally created by a group of Boston artists as a show-stopping finale to the city's Bicentennial celebrations, First Night has evolved into an intergenerational, interactive event that typically focuses on the arts and family fun. The name First Night was chosen because organizers didn't like the more negative but technically correct "Last Night." Official First Night International festivities incorporate the four pillars of community, celebration, the new year, and the arts into their activities. For more information on large-scale First Night events, visit http://www.firstnight.com.

Worship

Opening Song(s): Open your time together with 3–5 songs of praise and worship that reflect thankfulness for God's blessings, for God's continuing to walk with his people in all situations, and for hope for the future. Possibilities include "We Gather Together," "Be Thou My Vision," "Lead On, O King Eternal," "Not to Us," "Step by Step," "Revelation Song."

Scripture Reading: 2 Corinthians 5:16–6:10

Responsive Reading: paraphrase of Psalm 8

Leader: O Lord, Holy God, how majestic is your name in all the earth!

People: You have set your glory above the heavens.

Leader: Out of the mouths of babes and infants you have created a mighty fortress of protection against our enemies.

Program Focus: A faith-based New Year's Eve celebration

Key Verse: "If anyone is in Christ, there is a new creation: everything old has passed away; see, everything has become new!" (2 Corinthians 5:17 NRSV).

Purpose:
a. To review the year's highs and lows
b. To be in prayer—for self, family, the church, and the world
c. To create the "next step" in living out the new year according to God's will

People: When we look at your heavens, the work of your fingers, the moon and the stars that you have established, we have to ask, what are we human beings that you are mindful of us, mere mortals that you care for us?

Leader: The Lord our God has made us a little lower than God himself and crowned us with his glory and honor.

People: The Lord our God has made us caregivers of his creation, responsible for all other living things that he himself created.

Leader: People of God, as we celebrate the end of the old year and the beginning of the new, know that God has trusted us to do his work in this world, to care for creation, to care for God's children, to share the good news of Jesus Christ with this broken and hurting world.

People: May we, as God's people, be faithful to you, O Holy and Sovereign Lord. Let us walk with you and serve you with faith, hope, and love. Amen.

Time of Prayer: The worship leader should ask for worshipers to lift up joys and concerns they have as they prepare to start a new year. The leader can also pray with a focus on learning from our past and looking to the future with hope.

Closing Song: "Amazing Grace"

Note: Fellowship is a large part of the First Night program. Two formal stations are listed below that can accommodate larger groups. The third station will be the fellowship component.

Faith Stations

Station 1. Power of Prayer

What You'll Need

Volunteers: 3 station hosts plus 1 station host–song leader
Prayer walk supplies
Plastic tub (approximately 18" x 36" x 18" filled halfway with water)
Pile of smooth stones, 1 per person
Bath towel or tarp
Bibles
Length of mural paper with a mountains and valleys scene drawn on it
CD player and CD of the following songs: "I Love You Lord," "Create in Me a Clean Heart," "Spirit of the Living God," "Breathe," "Give Us Clean Hands,"
Words and music for the previous five songs (or prayer songs of your choosing)
Prayer posture photos (see note below)
Copies of the prayer walk map

Ahead of time, the planning team should create the prayer walk map. Choose four rooms to be the stops on the prayer walk. A station host will need to be at each stop, although the hosts take active roles only at Stop 2 (praying for groups, that God will be with them in the highs and lows of their lives) and Stop 3 (acting as a worship leader). The stops are as follows:

Stop 1. Lay Down Your Burdens

Set the plastic tub on the bath towel or tarp. Fill it half full with water. Set the pile of smooth stones and the Bibles next to the tub (put piles on all four sides to accommodate bigger groups). On the prayer walk map, identify the stop and give the following directions, remembering to talk softly so that you don't disturb others (adults will need to help the children):

Jesus tells us to lay down our burdens and he will carry our loads. Life is hard. What has been hard in your life this year? Read Matthew 11:28-30 quietly to yourself or your small group. Then pick up a stone. Feel its weight in your hand. Think about the burdens you've been carrying around this past year. What has hurt your heart? What has worried you?

What has weighed you down? Feel the weight of the stone. Look at it and see all of your burdens inside this stone. When you are ready, kneel by the tub and release your stone into the water. See it drop to the bottom. Look at your hand. It's empty. Jesus has those burdens now. Be at peace.

Stop 2. Mountains and Valleys

On the prayer walk map, identify the stop and give the following directions:

1. Look at the mountains and valleys scene. Think about your life this past year. What have been some high points, some mountaintop experiences, for you this year? Share them with your small group. What have been some low points, some valleys to walk through, this year? Share them with your small group.

2. When you are ready, choose one high point and write it or draw a picture of it on the mountains.

3. When you are ready, choose one low point and write it or draw a picture of it down in the valleys.

4. When your small group has finished, raise your hand. Your station host will come and pray for you, giving thanks that God is with you on the mountaintops and in the valleys of your lives.

Stop 3. Sing to the Lord a New Song

Identify the prayer walk stop on the map and give the following directions:

Sometimes our prayers are offered to God through our songs. The words we sing tell God what is in our hearts. Sometimes it is easier to let someone else's words do the talking. At this stop your station host will lead you in singing your prayers to God.

Note: The station host in this room will serve as a worship leader. He or she may opt to play guitar or piano instead of using the CD player. Also feel free to choose other songs more familiar to your congregation that can be used as sung prayers. Provide song sheets for the participants.

Stop 4. Prayer Postures

Identify the prayer walk stop on the map and give the following directions:

Sometimes it's helpful to use your body when you pray. Use a breath prayer and try out different postures. Some can be done individually; some can be done as a group. Try at least one new posture. The breath prayer is: (take a deep breath in as you say this phrase silently) "Lord Jesus Christ, have mercy on me" (now exhale as you say silently) "a sinner."

Posture A. Find your own space and sit with your eyes closed and face lifted heavenward while you say the prayer. Repeat several times.

Posture B. Find your own space and lie on the floor with your eyes closed while you say the prayer. Repeat several times.

Posture C. Find your own space and kneel while you say the prayer. Repeat several times.

Posture D. Find a small group of people, join hands, and say the prayer in unison. Repeat 3 times.

Posture E. Find a small group of people, stand in a circle, turn so that you are facing the next person's back, and put your hands on that person's shoulders. Now say the prayer in unison. Repeat 3 times.

Note: Ahead of time, the planning team can take digital photos of people doing the various prayer postures, print them, and tape them up around the station room.

Station 2. Resolutions and Re-formations

What You'll Need

Volunteer: station host
Copies of the 3-Minute Interview questions
Copies of My Resolutions handout (see below)
Large stainless steel bowl or small, portable charcoal grill
Matches
Candle
Paper butterflies preprinted with the words "Lord, please reform my heart so I can . . ."
Pens and pencils

The host should welcome participants to the station and ask them to gather in a semicircle. Pass out the 3-Minute Interview questions (taken from *Celebrate Good Times* by Elizabeth Crisci [Judson Press, 2005], 3) and ask adults to partner up with children who can't read yet. Participants can begin to move about the room finding others to interview. After one person/pair asks all the questions, the other person/pair may do the interview. Participants should write down the names of people they talk to. Keep time and ring a bell or otherwise signal when the 3 minutes are up and it's time to switch. Play this game for 15 minutes or so.

Elizabeth Crisci's suggested 3-Minute Interview questions are:

Where were you born?

What is your favorite snack food?

Who is your greatest hero/heroine?

What three words describe you?

What was the last good book you read or movie you saw?

Which Bible character are you most like (or is your favorite)?

What is your favorite hobby (or sport)?

If you had a day to do anything you wanted, what would you do?

Next, the host should direct people to take a seat at the tables. On the tables should be copies of the My Resolutions handout, the paper butterflies, and the pens and pencils. Explain that participants can complete the My Resolutions handout as a way of thinking about current behaviors they would like to change or new habits they would like to adopt for the new year. The handout is optional. Everyone, however, should take a butterfly and complete the statement with the one thing he or she most wants God to change. New Year's resolutions often fade away, but when we ask God to re-form our hearts and help us change our lives, his willpower makes a difference in our ability to succeed.

Give participants 5–10 minutes to work. When everyone has completed a butterfly, take the group outside and explain that the group is going to offer up these re-formation requests to God by burning them and letting the smoke float up to heaven. Say a brief prayer asking God to accept these offerings of the heart and then light a candle and touch the flame to each person's butterfly. As the butterfly begins to burn, the person can drop it into the stainless steel bowl where it should burn up. Or this can be done over and into a small charcoal grill. Adult supervision and assistance is required!

Note: To create the My Resolutions handout, type up the following acrostic and then type a blank acrostic below it (idea taken from Elizabeth Crisci's *Celebrate Good Times* [Judson Press, 2005], 5):

My Resolutions

N —No gossip

E —Entertain neighbor

W —Work harder

Y —Yearn to introduce others to Jesus

E —Expect answers to prayer

A —Apply the Bible more

R —Remember birthdays

N —

E —

W —

Y —

E —

A —

R —

Station 3. Party Time

What You'll Need

Volunteer: station host

Music

Board games

Group games played with TV/DVD player (such as "Are You Smarter Than a Fifth Grader?" or "Scene It")

Art supplies (play dough, Sculpey clay, Model Magic, watercolor paints and brushes, mosaic materials, mural paper, markers, etc.)

Ahead of time, the planning team should decide what type of art activities to have available. Consider purchasing some art packs online or at the local craft store or setting out materials to make the Paper Towel Tie-Dye or Tissue Paper Mosaic butterflies from the Dia de los Muertos program (see page 95) to tie in with the theme of renewal and re-formation. This extended fellowship time can also include music and food (see right).

Fellowship

If this program is being held on New Year's Eve, it may be starting after the dinner hour, so all the team will need to provide are snacks and drinks throughout the evening. However, the planning team may want to offer a make-your-own pizza activity during the fellowship time since this program may last for 4 or more hours, depending on the schedule.

For a fun, retro twist, the team may choose to serve popular/legendary snack foods that have been on the market for a while. Decorate the serving table with cutouts from the boxes or with nostalgic food ads found in old magazines or online. Note the inaugural year on a card by the dish. Possibilities include: Twinkies (1933), Pop Tarts (1964), Krispy Kreme Donuts (1937), Diet Coke (1982), Kool-Aid (1953), Betty Crocker Cake Mix (1937), Jelly Bellies (1978), and Jello Jigglers (1990) (idea taken from Elizabeth Crisci's *Celebrate Good Times,* Judson Press, 2005).